PARENTING IN THE AGE OF ATTENTION SNATCHERS

PARENTING IN THE AGE OF ATTENTION SNATCHERS

A Step-by-Step Guide to Balancing Your Child's Use of Technology

Lucy Jo Palladino, PhD

SHAMBHALA
BOSTON & LONDON
2015

Shambhala Publications, Inc.
Horticultural Hall
300 Massachusetts Avenue
Boston, Massachusetts 02115
www.shambhala.com

9 8 7 6 5 4 3 2 1

First Edition
Printed in the United States of America

♾ This edition is printed on acid-free paper that meets the
American National Standards Institute Z39.48 Standard.
♻ This book is printed on 30% postconsumer recycled paper.
For more information please visit www.shambhala.com.

Distributed in the United States by Penguin Random House LLC
and in Canada by Random House of Canada Ltd

Designed by Greta D. Sibley

Library of Congress Cataloging-in-Publication Data
Palladino, Lucy Jo.
Parenting in the age of attention snatchers: a step-by-step guide to balancing
your child's use of technology / Lucy Jo Palladino.—First edition.
pages cm
ISBN 978-1-61180-217-7 (paperback)
1. Parenting. 2. Attention in children. 3. Distraction (Psychology)
4. Technology and children. I. Title.
HQ755.8.P338 2015
306.874—dc23
2014031198

For Arthur, Julia, and Jennifer

Contents

Introduction

It was the best of times. It was the worst of times. Charles Dickens could easily have been talking about parenting in the twenty-first century.

It was the best of times. A mom I know was telling me that she and her family had gotten together with friends. The grown-ups visited, and the kids were on their iPads. "It felt so good to have some adult conversation without constantly getting interrupted, and the kids were doing what they wanted, too. It felt like a total win-win."

It was the worst of times. "Later on, I thought about it some more," she explained. "When I was a kid, I liked being in on grown-ups' conversations. . . . Are my kids learning it's OK to ignore other people? . . . Most of all, I worry about their brains."

It was the best of times. Every student can now access the world's storehouse of information. Preschoolers are reading-ready or already reading by the time they get to kindergarten. Kids use apps and social media to learn independently and stay connected with their friends.

It was the worst of times. As kids grow up attached to their devices, their attention spans for listening diminish. Attention problems proliferate. Digital media grabs kids' attention and doesn't let go of it easily.

Today's technology gives children powerful tools for a promising future. This same technology weakens their ability to pay attention without them, putting their future at risk.

INTO THE GREAT UNKNOWN

New technology finds its way into our homes faster than we can comprehend its effects on our families. For better or worse, it's altering our children's habits and brain development. With kids glued to their screens, it may appear that children today have more, not less, attention. But as you'll learn in chapter 2, attention that's captured (involuntary attention) is not the same as attention that's chosen (voluntary attention). *Involuntary attention,* like watching TV, and *voluntary attention,* like studying for a test, build different habits and different brain pathways.

The strength of your child's voluntary attention determines his future success. He needs it right now to control his use of technology. Attention snatchers—the digital devices that use high stimulation to grab your child's attention—can be friend or foe. To a child who can use them productively and turn them off, they are friend. To a child who cannot, they are foe.

ATTENTION

What will the world be like when our children reach our age? Will they work at jobs that haven't yet been invented? Will they be able to keep up? Since we don't know what lies ahead, how can we prepare our children to succeed? The answer lies with how we guide their budding ability to practice voluntary attention.

The lifelong benefits of attention learned in childhood cannot be overstated. Your child doesn't have to know what exact problem the future will bring, only how to give it his undivided attention. As a parent, you can be confident in your child's ability to succeed if you've raised him to control his own attention.

As your child navigates his way through life, if he gets stuck in a dark place emotionally—sad, hurt, angry, anxious, or afraid—if he can then withdraw his attention from his feelings of helplessness and redirect it to a more hopeful path, he can turn things around. He can adjust his attitude or mood from within.[1]

Voluntary attention is primary to your child's sense of purpose in life. He can stay true to the priorities he sets for himself. With it, he can listen and relate to others. Without it, he can be in your presence yet still be absent.

ONE MORE THING, REALLY?

As a parent, you have a right to feel frazzled. Because of technology, when you leave the office, you don't. You're still plugged into your job at home, where you're also a household manager, finance officer, chauffeur, chef, homework monitor, social director, and more.

I've been asked more than once, "Why do I need to teach my child to pay attention? No one had to teach me." It's true that parents have always had to set limits, but attention snatchers are game changers for raising kids today. As a child, you didn't have the same sensory overload your child has now. The only way your child can benefit from this overabundance of digital media is if she can become selective and self-controlled.

Your child's ability to use an off button is quite possibly the most important technological competency she can learn. You'll seldom get a bigger long-term payoff than when you invest the time to teach your child to control her attention. When she's no longer under your direct supervision, she'll still make good choices on her own.

Experts call this essential skill "cognitive control," another name for voluntary attention—which can also be called "impulse control," "delay of gratification," or just plain "self-control." In chapter 3, we'll discuss how children acquire and strengthen this ability at each stage in their development. Your toddler can do amazing things on an iPad, but what shapes her brain most at her age—what has the longest-lasting impact on her life—is what she learns when it's time to turn it off.

As we watch technology give rise to a new set of attention problems, we, as parents, need to do something that parents in past decades didn't have to think about: we need to help our children learn how to resist the distraction that their technology creates.

WHAT IF MY CHILD HAS ADHD?

This book is written for all parents, including those whose children have an attention disorder. Chapters 3 and 11 include some evidence-based considerations specifically for parents of kids with ADHD. (The medical designation for attention deficit disorder, with or without hyperactivity, is ADHD.[2])

If you have questions about the development of your child's attention, discuss them with his doctor. This book is designed to provide helpful information, but it doesn't take the place of professional health care for your child.

IN THE CHAPTERS AHEAD

Parenting in the Age of Attention Snatchers covers problems and solutions for raising children from birth to young adulthood to balance the use of their technology. It has three parts:

Part One. This book is research-based, and part one gives you clear explanations of the science that supports it. You'll appreciate the steps in part two, and be better able to put them into practice, when you understand their foundations.

Part Two. Here you'll find the seven steps to teach children to pay attention, along with specific suggestions and practical tips.

Part Three. To help you put the seven steps into practice, the final chapters take a closer look at attention snatchers and ways to help your child strengthen his self-control.

In the back of the book, you'll find a Notes section with chapter-by-chapter citations and an index.

If Charles Dickens were alive today, I imagine he'd wonder how, with the power and wonder of technology, we could be living in anything other than the best of times. But then again, he understood human nature pretty well. A century and a half ago, he observed, "Electric communication will never be a substitute for the face of someone who with their soul encourages another person to be brave and true."

PART ONE

Technology, Attention, and Your Child's Brain

Part one explains the science behind the seven steps in part two. You'll be more effective at the steps, and put them into action faster, too, if you understand how and why they work.

Chapter 1 shows how your child's ability to control his attention is the single most important predictor of his success at school, work, and life, and also provides insights about attention control.

Chapter 2 describes the critical difference between *voluntary* attention, which requires effort, and *involuntary* attention, which is captured by a screen.

Chapter 3 gives you essential information about the way your child's brain grows: what to look for and how to support each developmental stage so that your child will build strong voluntary attention.

These informational chapters describe highlights of relevant, new research. I've also included some interesting details for these references in the Notes section (in the back of the book).

1

A Parent's Dilemma

Before I got married I had six theories about raising children. Now I have six children and no theories.

—John Wilmot

Not long ago, in a *New York Times* article, former technology reporter David Pogue described his quandry as the parent of a six-year-old who spends hours on an iPad:

> I'm doing a lot of thinking lately. Is a gadget automatically bad for our children just because it's electronic? What if it's fostering a love of music, an affinity for theater, and expertise in strategy and problem-solving? Is it a bad thing for a kid to be so much in love with mental exercises? Am I really being a good parent by yanking THAT away?[1]

Then, Pogue continued with an equally compelling argument against his own line of reasoning. He observed that his son gets "bizarrely upset when I say I have to take it away now—out-of-character upset . . . Having read the *New York Times* series on the physiological effects of electronics on young minds, I'm plenty worried."

I hear about this struggle time and again from parents. Kids today have a world of possibility, power, and pleasure at their fingertips, while their parents face the dilemma of our age: let your kid play with digital media and feel guilty, or take it away and feel guilty, too.

YOU ARE NOT ALONE

I'm writing this chapter seated on a plane behind two families who began this trip as strangers. Their children range in age from about three to ten years old. The parents have struck up a conversation: "Yeah, they're something, aren't they? I feel like we were doing OK until we got DVD in the back seats." (The adults laugh knowingly.) "It opened Pandora's box . . ."

I could pretty much piece together how this conversation began, a scene unfolding on other planes and in restaurants and waiting rooms—children playing with digital devices, their parents comparing notes. They remind me of travelers in a foreign land who come across someone else from their own country. They exchange stories and tips, ask each other questions, feel validated and reassured, and continue on their adventure.

When we check with others, we feel a sense of normalcy about our own choices, even though we know that what's right for the family in row 8 may not be right for us. Each child is different, the same child has different needs at different ages, and kids use technology in different ways for different reasons. No set of rules about screentime can provide all the answers, and the questions change as quickly as the technology we're using.

We want to give our children all that technology has to offer. It's their future. But we worry about a hidden pay-me-later factor that won't be ignored or dismissed. This nagging sense of doubt about raising the touchscreen generation has been dubbed "the neurosis of our age."[2]

I hear many versions:

> I'm a mom, and a teacher, too. As a mom, I want my child to be ahead of the curve. He's got a real knack for this kind of thing. But as a teacher, I don't think it's right, the way he gets glued to the screen.

> She's a good kid, but when she pulls out her phone and answers texts when we're talking, it hurts my feelings. I don't say anything because all the other kids do it, and I've got to pick my battles.

> I know he spends too much time playing video games, but he doesn't make friends easily, and this is his way of relating to the other boys.

I don't see this inner conflict as a neurosis. I see it as a healthy sign that parents want to weigh potential benefits and costs, and they see that their children already belong to a world where facility with technology is a must.

Sometimes it's hard to remember that as a parent, you have good reason to trust yourself. No one knows your child like you do, and no one else has more at stake, except your child. This is useful to remember in a tense moment when you need the conviction to say "Stop!" as your child screams "No!" Your child's future-self will be appreciative, but his present-day-self—not so much. At moments like that, every parent feels alone.

I encourage parents to replace their guilt with caution, and to use that caution as a sign that they need more information—not just from the family in row 8 but also from a cross section of credible sources. That's why I wrote this book.

THE NEW NEED FOR AN OLD IDEA

More than ever, we can learn from a landmark study conducted in the late 1960s and early 1970s at Stanford University, called "the marshmallow test."[3] Psychologist Walter Mischel carried out a series of experiments in which he offered young children an immediate small reward, such as a marshmallow, or twice the reward if they'd wait fifteen minutes to receive it.

Follow-up studies showed that children who waited longer for their treats fared better in later life, including better SAT scores, educational achievement, response to stress, long-term friendships, body mass index (BMI), and more. The children were tracked at various intervals until they were forty years old. At every age, the marshmallow test of self-control predicted future success more accurately than any other measure, including IQ.

Mischel recounts the details of his original studies in *The Marshmallow Test*. Each preschooler was observed individually through a one-way mirror. The child sat on a chair at a table with a red button that summoned the experimenter to re-enter the room. The child and adult practiced with the button so that the child could see that the adult kept his word. Then the adult left the child alone with an attractive treat that the child had chosen from a tray of goodies. (Beforehand, Mischel had run informal studies to identify which treats four-year-olds craved the most, which turned out to be marshmallows, cookies, and pretzel sticks.)

Each child wrestled with the task. A few ate their treats the moment the experimenter left the room. Some closed their eyes; others stared at the treat. One child carefully removed the chocolate cookie layer of an Oreo, licked the white icing, and put the cookie back.

The majority of children held out for an average of three minutes before eating their treats, but 30 percent of them waited the full fifteen minutes and received double the reward. Their tactics varied. Some covered their eyes with their hands or played hide-and-seek under their desks. Others sang songs. In several of the studies, Mischel suggested specific mental techniques to the children, such as "think fun thoughts."

Mischel concluded that the crucial skill for success was "strategic allocation of attention." High delayers—those who waited longest for their treats—were able to withdraw their attention from the "hot stimulus" and deliberately redirect it elsewhere.

VOLUNTARY ATTENTION: AN ESSENTIAL AND ENDANGERED ABILITY

What would happen if four-year-olds today were left alone in a room for fifteen minutes with what they crave the most—their twenty-first-century marshmallow, an iPad with their favorite app? How easily would they cave in, accustomed only to a world in which waiting is outdated?

The skill that Mischel identified as "strategic allocation of attention" goes by various names: delay of gratification, impulse control, suppression, self-discipline, voluntary attention, top-down attention. Many experts call it "cognitive control." I like the term "voluntary attention," as it names what Mischel observed: success depends on a child's effort to control her own attention. As the marshmallow test showed, cognitive control—voluntary attention—sends ripples far into your child's future.

Studies similar to the marshmallow test have reconfirmed the ability of voluntary attention to predict a child's long-term success. A longitudinal study of thirteen-year-olds in Pennsylvania, published in 2005, found that cognitive control was twice as influential as IQ in predicting future grades and admissions to selective schools.[5] In 2011, researchers in New Zealand published the results of a long-term study in which they tested and tracked more than a thousand children, ages three to twelve. Those who developed greater cognitive control in childhood were in better physical health and had greater financial success at thirty-two years of age.[6]

Apps are a fun, effective way for your child to learn reading and math skills. But the lesson your child learns when it's time to turn off her iPad will influence her future more profoundly than will learning new words or times tables. Cognitive control is the hub for all other learning skills.

Children today face an unprecedented challenge to their cognitive control—namely, attention snatchers. Computers, tablets, smartphones, TVs, and game consoles open new worlds of information, skill-building, and enjoyment for kids. But they do so by providing an endless stream of novelty and stimulation that *captures* their attention. Attention that's captured is called "involuntary attention." To build cognitive control, a child needs to exercise *effort* to pay attention, which is why it's called "voluntary attention." (We'll discuss involuntary and voluntary attention in chapter 2.) If she depends on a screen to pay attention, your child is weakening this essential ability. What's more, her young brain is malleable. Weakening or strengthening her voluntary attention now has lasting effects.

At the right time and place, an attention snatcher is a friend. If your grade-schooler hates history, you want the History Channel to capture her attention. Or if your college freshman excels at math but not spatial intelligence, playing action games that teach 3-D mental rotation can help her become an engineer or an architect. Way to go, attention snatchers!

But if your grade-schooler can't turn the TV off or your college student is up late gaming every night, then their attention snatchers are taking more than they give. They're stealing your child's cognitive control, putting her future at risk.

We're constantly balancing the yin and yang of life—ice cream now or look good in jeans later; a shopping spree today or a new car next year. Children need to balance their yin and yang, too—chat online all night or study and ace a test tomorrow. But attention snatchers have thrown this yin and yang out of balance, especially for our children. They don't yet have the capacity to weigh future consequences, and now they hold a device in their hands that instantly delivers compelling sensory stimulation—the quintessential shiny metal object. Attention snatchers tip the scales in the direction of immediate rewards.

Nobel laureate Daniel Kahneman tells us that true happiness is a balance of feeling happy moment-by-moment and feeling happy when you think about your life, which is called "life satisfaction." He bases this definition on research about the way that the brain works.[7] We have a self who experiences life and a self who remembers it. The self who experiences life seeks happiness right now; the self who remembers it seeks life satisfaction. Our brains are built so that we're happiest not when we constantly seek happiness but when we balance it with purpose, achieving meaningful goals, and feeling like we're living the best lives we can.

We want our children to be happy and also to feel satisfied with their life choices, so we need to guide the development of their cognitive control. They'll always be able to eat a marshmallow right away. But if they don't have the ability to wait and get two later, they're missing what they need for a truly happy life.

A CHILD'S BRAIN IS A MIRACLE

Children's behavior can be puzzling, even maddening at times. You need endless repetition to teach your child to say "thank you," but let an expletive slip out just once, and your child says it every day.

Why do kids pick up on some behaviors and not others? Their brains seek stimulation—and children's apps deliver. They incorporate amusement, surprise, immediate feedback, variable rewards, and challenges at different levels by offering unlockable extras. In fact, *their goal is to weaken children's ability to resist*. Not for nothing is the tagline to the app Amazing Ants: "*Addictive* Physics-Based Gameplay" (italics mine).

Strong sensory stimuli—video games, Internet surfing, texting, social networking—are powerful external motivators for adults, too, but children are especially vulnerable. Their immature brains offer weak resistance to novel sights and sounds. Plus, their brain pathways are growing quickly. When a habit takes hold, it has lasting power.

When you were a child, did you speak a foreign language or learn to play a musical instrument or a sport? With a bit of practice (and a sense of humor), you can return to it as an adult. It's extraordinary, really: skills learned in childhood become so deeply rooted that they influence the range of choices we'll have all our lives.

As a parent, you carry the weight of this responsibility on your shoulders. Suppose you overlook a skill your child will need later in life or place too much importance on one skill at the price of another. When should you allow your child to play with an iPad, engaging in mental exercise and developing greater facility with technology, and when should you stop him, so he develops the ability to walk away from it?

DUST OR MAGIC?

For years, on the first Sunday of November, designers of children's interactive media gathered in Lambertville, New Jersey, for a meeting called "Dust or Magic." Attendance grew and the demand became global. Today, Dust or Magic holds classes, conferences, and camps throughout the year in many cities. I like the name. "Dust" means an app is boring. "Magic" means it's stimulating enough to capture a child's attention.

What I like most about the name is that it alerts us to remember how magic works. A skillful magician diverts our attention, so while we look in one place, we miss what's happening somewhere else. While we marvel at ingenious apps for teaching kids language arts, math, and science, we miss how their compelling sights and sounds accustom our children to involuntary attention. These apps activate the reward centers in our children's brains so strongly that our kids don't want to stop playing.

The designers at Dust or Magic are good magicians, not bad guys. Many encourage the intentional use of iPads by children, a sensible practice we'll discuss later in this book. They know better than most that when an app is so stimulating that it captivates, it's also so stimulating that it can condition a child to crave more.

AWARENESS IS KRYPTONITE TO ATTENTION SNATCHERS

As everyone's screentime increases, we need awareness to keep it in check. We need to train ourselves to ask the question, "What am I *not* doing now?" Asking yourself what you're *not* doing, or *not* looking at, or *not* thinking about, serves as a self-reminder to stop browsing and go for a walk, read a book, or tackle the boring job you've been avoiding. This type of awareness is called a "metacognition," or taking a step back to think about your thinking.

We don't use the *word* "metacognition" every day, but we do use metacognitions every day. It's how we self-correct. Let's say you discover that your child has a much earlier or later bedtime than her friends. You start to wonder if your rule is too strict or too lenient, influenced more by feelings about your own upbringing than your child's present-day needs. You adjust her bedtime. That's a metacognition. You've examined the nature of your own thinking and revised your decision accordingly.

Metacognition is self-awareness that requires self-observation and self-honesty. Brain-imaging (MRI) studies have linked metacognition to activity in the newest part of the brain, a region at the very front called the "anterior prefrontal cortex."[8] This specific region is one of the few parts of the brain with anatomical properties that are unique to humans. René Descartes might conclude, "I think about thinking, therefore I am human."

Using metacognition to promote awareness helps us stay true to our long-term goals and restore the balance of our yin and yang. If we get obsessed with ice cream, shopping, or binge TV, and ask ourselves the question, "What am I *not* thinking about now?" the neurons in our anterior prefrontal cortex start to fire. They reconnect us with our commitments to weight-watching, saving, or staying physically active.

One of our most important long-term goals for our children needs to be the development of their voluntary attention. The more voluntary attention they have, the happier their lives (and ours) will be. We need to make sure this goal doesn't get derailed by an attention snatcher. Until they're old enough, we need to exercise metacognition for them: "What is my child *not* doing now?" As they mature, we need to help them learn metacognition for themselves.

The 30 percent of children who succeeded in the marshmallow test used rudimentary, early childhood versions of metacognition. Mischel noted that many children started out trying to stare their marshmallow down. When they realized this approach was not helping, they reversed tactics and turned their focus away. Had they not been trying to resist a temptation, they wouldn't have discovered how to outsmart a hot stimulus like that. Mischel urges parents to establish rules and rituals so kids can figure out how to make themselves wait and exercise self-awareness.

METACOGNITION: BALANCING THE PROMISE *AND* THE RISK

If you feel yourself getting swept up by either the exciting benefits or the harmful pitfalls that new technology brings, use it as a cue to put yourself on pause. It's time to practice metacognition about technology and assess both its promise and its risk. When technology is truly innovative, though, its promise is alluring and its risk can be hidden.

Like many of my colleagues, I watched with interest when iPads were introduced and children demonstrated an instant affinity for using them. Very young children are biologically primed for touchscreens. They learn with their hands and are especially drawn to the power of producing lights and sounds with them. Remember when your child was a baby and you held her in your arms while standing next to a wall that had a light switch? Do you recall the look on her face when she reached out and discovered she could turn the lights on and off? The entire room was at her command! . . . until you moved and the light switch was out of her reach. But a touchscreen can sit on *her* lap and do so much more. At Dust or Magic, they call the iPad a rattle on steroids.

As iPads caught on, I was filled with enthusiasm about their potential as educational tools. High-quality, interactive, digital textbooks give older children an information-rich multimedia experience at the exact moment they're pursuing a particular question or interest. The stimulation of their senses keeps them motivated, and the fact that they're in charge keeps them involved. I bought my iPad immediately after previewing the interactive version of E. O. Wilson's *Life on Earth*, which enabled me to visualize and appreciate the intricacies of DNA replication for the first time in my life. I imagined what it would be like to see this as a science-minded middle-schooler.

With touchscreens, children can learn at their own pace, explore a vast range of interests, became facile with technology at early ages, share media adventures with friends and family, and have fun!

All true, but do I sound one-sided? That's what I mean by sensing imbalance and using it as a cue to step back and ask: "What am I *not* thinking about here?" Is there risk as well as promise? If a science-minded middle-schooler has a future in medicine or biotechnology, her years of rigorous training will require painstaking patience. What lies ahead for her when she doesn't understand a concept right away? She'll need endurance for when answers are not forthcoming, and perseverance and motivation from within. She needs to build the willpower to wait—the opposite of the touchscreen experience.

Most researchers and educators agree that kids need hands-on experience with materials, people, and nature. As child-development expert Nancy Carlsson-Paige points out, "Open-ended materials such as blocks, play dough, art and building materials, sand, and water encourage children to play creatively and in-depth. Neuroscience tells us that as children play this way, connections and pathways to the brain become activated and solidify."[9]

Does this mean our children should stop using touchcreens? Of course not. That would be the same mistake in the other direction—seeing only the risk while losing sight of the promise. Most of the jobs in the future will be technology-driven. You want your child to be competent and confident with digital media.

The goal of metacognition is to balance the risk *and* the promise. For instance, after you notice that you've been overlooking how much time your child spends on an iPad, you can create more opportunities for playing dress-up, using modeling clay and building toys, or constructing forts with blankets and furniture. Many young touchscreeners will take to this easily; others will resist—in which case, you may be headed for mud pies and rocketry to compete with the captivating pull of apps. Later in the book, we'll discuss individual differences among children, and why some are more strongly attracted to screens than others.

IN THE PILOT'S SEAT

One afternoon, I was speaking to a large audience of parents. I'd come to a part in my presentation where I discuss studies that link TV watching and attention problems in children (which you'll read about in chapter 11). A woman raised her hand and when she stood up, she loudly denounced the studies, claiming they proved nothing. Before I had the chance to respond, she stormed out of the room.

When my presentation was over, the woman returned to apologize. She said she was surprised by her own outburst. She explained that as a single mom, she worked long hours to support her son, and she knew he watched too much TV during his preschool years. Recently, as a fourth grader, he'd been diagnosed with ADHD. Hearing me talk about these studies had stirred up feelings of blame and guilt. "I'm tired of everyone thinking it's my fault." Her anger turned into tears.

I thanked her for returning and explaining. We sat and talked as she regained her composure. We discussed the strong genetic component in ADHD, how the diagnosis can mean different things, and how each child is unique. She shared with me how hard her son's preschool years had been for her, how every day she yearned to spend more time with him, and how deeply it hurt her still, just thinking about it.

I told her how being a parent is a lot like being a pilot, having to take multiple, critical factors into account to keep your plane in the air. It's an analogy I've used many times in my practice, as it aptly describes how a parent has to appreciate all the conditions that impact her family. I told her that her son was lucky to have a mother who was a caring and determined pilot. She smiled for a moment but went on to say how she knew that others—even her own family—blamed her for her son's ADHD. I reminded her that no one from the ground is in a position to criticize the woman in the pilot's seat.

BE AWARE OF YOUR OWN BIAS

When that mother stood up to denounce the studies I was presenting, her criticism wasn't based on their merits but on the painful feelings they evoked in her. To return to the airplane analogy, it would be like declaring that an instrument in the cockpit isn't working, not because you have hard evidence but because you don't like what it says or you're afraid to look.

We all discredit information because we wish it weren't true, and like the hard-working mom in my audience, we aren't aware that we're doing it when we do. Research psychologists have found that the way our brains work causes us to have certain biases in how we think and react. This woman was demonstrating a bias known as "cognitive dissonance." We tend to filter for evidence that supports our own choices and opinions, so our brains don't have to endure the dissonance or inner conflict caused by contradictory information. Then we surround ourselves with people who share our own views.

This bias occurs, for example, when parents who are gamers discount findings that children who frequently play video games are less attentive at school. Instead, they favor studies that show that video games teach children useful skills such as strategy and spatial intelligence. Nongamers, however, are more inclined to see the value in studies that link gaming to school problems and to dismiss studies that show that gaming teaches skills.

If we try, we can use self-observation to keep cognitive dissonance in check. To some degree, we can compensate for it by: (1) knowing it exists; (2) knowing what our bias is likely to be; and (3) applying metacognition—the "What am I *not* thinking about?" question. Be as detached as you can be, as if you were asked to debate both sides of the issue.

It's easier to see another person's bias than your own—as in the game of "blind man's bluff" poker, where players place their cards on their foreheads and each player sees everyone else's cards except his own. In fact, many times, without realizing it, we use the act of noticing other people's biases as a way of *not* noticing our own. Honestly answering the question, "What am *I* not looking at now?" can be surprisingly informative.

PARENTING WITHOUT FEAR

The topic of children's use of technology can be a hot button. We care deeply about being responsible parents, we're in uncharted territory, and we don't want our children to miss out. (In chapter 11, we'll talk about FOMO, the fear of missing out.)

The hard-working mom at my presentation was upset recalling how, in order to earn a living, she couldn't spend more time with her son. In today's world, her plight is far from uncommon. If you're like most parents, you're trying to make ends meet, provide for your family, and save for your children's college education. You work long hours both on the job and at home. Many times, your children's screentime makes life possible because there aren't enough hours in the day for you to be with them any more than you already are. The fear of being expected to do more than is humanly possible can cause a parent to be biased against information that raises questions about screentime.

Also, like many parents, you may be afraid that speaking up will lead to a confrontation, especially if your child has a strong personality and it's time for her to turn off her iPad. Understandably, we all want peace in our homes and we need to prioritize issues. But sometimes important problems get swept under the rug because we're afraid to face them. It happens to parents everywhere. Your child's voluntary attention may be a top priority, but its long-term payoff is not immediately evident, so it's easy to let it slide.

Another fear, especially when parenting teens who are tech-savvy, is that you'll sound old, irrelevant, and uncool if you say what's really on your mind. Our thinking brain gets silenced because our emotional brain doesn't want our kids to mock us. Many children are quicker than their parents at adapting to the next new thing, but they still need adult guidance, now more than ever. They're not yet seasoned with life experience.

We make better decisions when we base them on fact, not fear. And making fact-based decisions sets a good example for our growing children as well.

So much of our children's future lies beyond our control. We need to control what we can, and we *can* teach our children self-control. As the marshmallow test showed, children who control their own attention are on a trajectory to succeed in life.

In the next chapter, I'll describe the critical difference between voluntary and involuntary attention and why telling the two apart is indispensable when it comes to preventing attention snatchers from taking over.

2

What Is Voluntary Attention?

The essential achievement of will is
to attend to a difficult object.
—William James

Why can your child pay rapt attention to his favorite TV show but fail to listen to a simple set of directions? It's because each task requires a different kind of attention and a different type of brain activity. Watching TV engages *involuntary* attention, and following directions requires *voluntary* attention.

INVOLUNTARY AND VOLUNTARY ATTENTION

We use labels for different kinds of attention—selective, sustained, focused, unfocused, divided, undivided, continuous, partial, to name a few. Each describes attention as it would appear to an onlooker. In this chapter, we'll use names that are based on neural pathways—attention as it appears from the brain's point of view.[1]

The term "involuntary attention" comes from the fact that it requires no effort. Involuntary attention is ongoing. It *involuntarily* follows the strongest stimulus that captures it. To some degree, we're in this state all the time, ready to be drawn to the most stimulating sights and sounds.

When your child is captivated by the exploits of SpongeBob SquarePants, he's in a passive, receptive mode. His attention is controlled by an external stimulus and mostly *involuntary*. The sights and sounds of a bright yellow sea sponge successfully attract the part of his brain called the "sensory cortex." SpongeBob and his pals stir emotion, so your child's emotionally responsive limbic system wants him to stay put and watch. For the most part, he's reacting to SpongeBob, not acting on his own behalf.

The term "voluntary attention" comes from the fact that effort is required. You pay attention *voluntarily*, on purpose, or it doesn't happen. Voluntary attention goes by other names, as well. In the marshmallow test, Mischel called it "strategic allocation of attention" when he identified it as the key to a child's success. As we discussed in chapter 1, some scientists call it "cognitive control." Others call it "top-down attention," after the brain pathways that support it.[2] The words "voluntary attention" can be helpful because they pinpoint its two critical components: you need to *volunteer* your effort to direct your *attention*.

Let's say you're helping your child with his homework. You ask him to create a new document, type in a heading, answer three review questions, and save his work. When you check on him twenty minutes later, he's staring at a blank screen or chatting online. Your directions require him to actively take charge and use his *voluntary* attention. To succeed, he has to intentionally direct and maintain his own focus. He needs to activate a part of his brain called the "prefrontal cortex," located in the front of the head, closest to the forehead. For the most part, he must act upon, not react to, sensory stimuli. He needs to choose to exert his own mental energy from within.

Involuntary and voluntary attention have these important differences:

ATTENTION	
Involuntary	**Voluntary**
Passive	Active
Stimulus-driven (originates with stimuli)	Self-directed (originates with effort)
Reactive	Volitional (willful)
Reflexive (determined by properties of objects)	Intentional (determined by your own goals)
Impulsive, cued	Deliberate
Is captured	Is allocated
Ongoing	By effort only

Involuntary attention involves older parts of the brain and helped our ancestors survive. It attracts us to food, mating, status, power, and emotion, and it alerts us to potential danger. That's why it's ongoing. Our survival could depend on our ability to react immediately to an urgent sight or sound.

Our attention involuntarily follows a "hot" stimulus, such as a dessert tray, a hundred-dollar bill, the sound of our own name, or any new or unusual sights or sounds that stir the senses or evoke emotion. In today's world, Twitter, Instagram, Vine, Snapchat, Facebook, online chatting, texting, TV, YouTube, movies, and video games of all genre, to name a few, are hot stimuli.

Voluntary attention originates in newer parts of the brain and helps us achieve our goals. It's an act of will—a conscious choice to pay attention to this and not that. Examples include attentiveness in class, reading a book, playing an instrument, concentrating in sports, and listening carefully to another person even if your cell phone starts to ring.

To a greater or lesser degree, the sights and sounds on screens trigger involuntary attention, while schoolwork and meaningful relationships require voluntary attention. Emma, age four, can stay focused on her iPad for hours but gets restless in preschool at circle time. Ten-year-old Sam concentrates when he plays video games but doesn't listen at the dinner table and bolts as soon as he can. Ben, age fourteen, answers texts immediately but doesn't study for exams until 11 P.M. the night before. That's because iPad apps, video games, and texts capture involuntary attention, while circle time, listening at the dinner table, and studying require voluntary attention.

Sitting still without a screen—at school, at the dinner table, or at a desk to do homework—requires mental effort, especially to get started. The brain will register cues that say it's time to begin, such as moving into place around the circle, sitting down at the table, or opening a textbook. But these cues don't compel your child to pay attention the way that novel stimuli from a screen do.

Once at a screen, your child exercises some voluntary attention, depending on his activity. For example, when he plays a video game such as *Minecraft*, he's using voluntary attention to figure out what to build and how to build it. But his interest is driven by onscreen cues, so although his attention is voluntary, it's not as effortful and it's being conditioned to need high stimulation.

For most human activity, we engage in both involuntary *and* voluntary attention at practically the same time. How much of each is a matter of degree. Suppose your child is engaged in involuntary attention, watching the latest exploits of SpongeBob. Something reminds him of a character from a previous episode and he intentionally tries to remember the character's name. He exerts effort, an act of voluntary attention.

Similarly, suppose your child is exerting voluntary attention, doing his homework. A color photo in his textbook catches his eye and triggers an idea for one of his answers. Although completing homework is primarily an act of voluntary attention, his involuntary attention kicked in to help.

We're at our best when our involuntary and voluntary attention work together as a team. Let's say that one of your goals is to find a summer camp for your child. You exercise voluntary attention, with some help from involuntary attention, by going online, searching, and gathering information from websites. Later that day, waiting for your child to finish dance class, you vaguely overhear two other parents talking on the far end of the room. The phrase "awesome camp" pops out and summons your involuntary attention. You walk over and use your voluntary attention to enter the conversation, and can now pursue this lead, as well.

THE ROLE OF ATTENTIONAL WEIGHT

Another way to understand the relationship between involuntary and voluntary attention is to understand what scientists call "attentional weight."[3] Every sight and sound around you has a different attentional weight *for you*. The stimulus with the most attentional weight is the one you pay attention to.

The attentional weight of any sight and sound depends on:

1. *The inherent properties of the stimulus*—for instance, how loud, bright, novel, fascinating, primal, or easily accessed it is.
2. *The strength of your voluntary attention*—which, in turn, depends on
    - How practiced you are at effortful attention and how much you've built up those brain pathways.
    - The aptitudes you were born with.
    - Situational factors, especially how well-rested, well-nourished, and well-exercised you are.
    - Temporary factors, especially how exhausted your self-control is from resisting other distractions.

3. *The importance of your goal to you*—a high-priority goal will motivate you to exert more effort to pay attention.

The attentional weight of an activity is different at different times. As an example, let's consider this question: which has more attentional weight for your nine-year-old this afternoon, watching TV or doing homework? Let's apply the three key elements:

1. *The inherent properties of the stimulus*. No contest. SpongeBob wins. Review questions lose.
2. *The strength of your nine-year-old's voluntary attention*. Weaker than yours. As we'll discuss in the next chapter, a nine-year-old's brain is immature, and the part of his brain that's the least developed are the pathways he needs for voluntary attention. How does his voluntary attention compare to that of other nine-year-olds? That depends on
   - How much he's practiced voluntary attention in the first nine years of his life—for instance, reading and studying instead of watching TV.
   - His genetic predisposition, which we'll discuss in the next chapter.
   - How much sleep, good nutrition, and physical exercise he's had.
   - How long he's been using his voluntary attention without a break and whether it's temporarily depleted.
3. *The importance of his goal to him*. Does he want a good grade? Does he want you to feel proud of him? Does he want to feel proud of himself? Has he connected the dots between homework and these goals? On the other hand, does he need to alter his mood right now with TV? Does he care what happens to SpongeBob? How much does he want to be included in the conversation if his friends talk about this episode tomorrow?

The reason we make rules for nine-year-olds, like homework first and then TV, is because the attentional weight of distraction is stacked up against them. But they won't be nine-year-olds for long, and we need to help them make good choices on their own. We do this by helping them build voluntary attention and connecting the dots between today's actions and tomorrow's goals.

BOTTOM-UP AND TOP-DOWN BRAIN PATHWAYS

Brain researchers have identified two main attention networks in the brain: "bottom-up" pathways that support involuntary attention, and "top-down" pathways that support voluntary attention.[4] In other words, if you could see inside your child's head, when his involuntary attention is engaged watching SpongeBob SquarePants, his bottom-up pathways light up. And when he engages in voluntary attention to do his homework, he activates top-down pathways.

Bottom-up neural pathways are so named because, primarily, they travel from older parts of the brain that are responsible for sensory experience *up* to newer ones that are responsible for thought. And for the most part, top-down neural pathways travel *down* from the newer, thinking parts of the brain to older, sensory ones. Most activities involve at least some involuntary and voluntary attention, activating both sets of neural pathways to a greater or lesser extent.

When the TV is on, bottom-up pathways fire inside your child's brain. If the on-screen action is startling, these pathways originate in the brain stem. If the story is suspenseful, his limbic system is involved. If the screen bursts with vivid color, sound effects, and jingles, his sensory cortex lights up.

The purpose of bottom-up pathways is to alert your child and orient him toward incoming stimuli, so neural reactivity is fast and effortless. Humans have a natural tendency to use bottom-up pathways because they conserve energy. Bottom-up pathways are the paths of least resistance.

In contrast, if we could peek inside your child's brain as he sits at his desk doing homework, we'd see neurons firing from his prefrontal cortex down to the lower regions of his brain. These top-down pathways direct his attention to sensory cues in his word processing document and textbook.

The prefrontal cortex is the seat of "executive functions"—planning, decision making, reasoning, abstract thought, and voluntary attention—and it requires effort to initiate these processes. The hardest part is getting started. We have to turn our own power buttons on. The following chart compares bottom-up and top-down neural circuits.

BRAIN PATHWAYS	
Bottom-Up	**Top-Down**
Involuntary attention	Voluntary attention
Originates from sensory cortices and brain stem ***up*** to prefrontal cortex	Originates from prefrontal cortex ***down*** to sensory cortices and brain stem
Fast	Slow
Effortless	Effortful
Alerts and orients	Executive functions

BOTTOM-UP PATHWAYS CAN BE HELPFUL OR UNHELPFUL

It's a thing of beauty to watch figure skaters perform at the Olympics, a chess master play multiple boards, or musicians improvise spontaneously. As a result of many years of concentrated practice, they can now depend on their fast, effortless bottom-up pathways to collaborate elegantly with their top-down network.

Before reaching this stage of mastery, experts begin, like anyone else, with a deliberate effort to learn the basics. They exercise strong voluntary attention to practice and improve their skills. The more they do this, the more that their training carries attentional weight for them. They become attracted to their own practice of correct action and sequences. They repeat their routines with conscious effort until they no longer need top-down pathways to direct the actions they've practiced repeatedly. Then they can rely on their faster bottom-up pathways to orient them automatically to make correct decisions and movements.

Brain-imaging studies point to the way that the brain accomplishes this.[5] When subjects successfully ignore distracters, response suppression is evident in the sensory cortex, which would otherwise show brain activity for involuntary attention. In other words, top-down pathways result in both increased attentional weight for cues that help you achieve your goal *and* decreased attentional weight for cues that don't. The more you focus with top-down pathways on the things that count, the more help you get from your bottom-up pathways to ignore the things that don't.

Of course, the opposite is true, as well. Untrained bottom-up pathways go rogue. With weak voluntary attention and no meaningful goals, bottom-up pathways will lead your child to the hottest stimuli in his environment, and those pathways of distraction will strengthen over time, too.

As the French writer Michel de Montaigne once observed, "No wind favors he who has no destined port." Bottom-up neural pathways go one step further, casting your attention in the direction of the strongest wind in any direction. From time to time, relaxing in this state can be a boost to creativity, but only if you return to the course you've set for yourself toward your goals.

Today, in the twenty-first century, involuntary attention is getting swept away by gale-force wind—the power of digital media to attract bottom-up pathways—especially for children. Their prefrontal cortex—the origin of top-down pathways in the brain—is not yet fully developed, which makes them more vulnerable than adults to react to hot stimuli. When it comes to attention snatchers, what's critical for us to understand is that digital media is capable of usurping the power of bottom-up networks in children's brains that were meant to help them reach their goals.[6]

THE ROLE OF DOPAMINE IN BUILDING HABITS

The functions of the brain chemical dopamine are complicated and not fully understood, but one known link is with reward and motivation. When you're rewarded for your efforts, you want to try even more. It's like riding a bicycle. Moving yourself forward makes it easier to keep moving forward, and in the brain, that's due to a sustainable supply of dopamine.

If your child sits down to do her homework and makes a deliberate effort and gets going, soon she'll gain momentum. Dopamine pumps through her brain at just the right pace.

Dopamine fuels champion skaters, chess masters, and skilled musicians to put in the years of practice needed for their bottom-up pathways to support their goals. Their continuing efforts produce success, which produces dopamine, which rewards their continuing efforts, which continue to produce more success. At the right pace, dopamine is the biologic mediator of "Nothing succeeds like success."

But getting started on homework can be slow and difficult for a child at the end of a school day. It's as if she's got to start pedaling that bicycle on the sharp incline of a hill. Meanwhile, the mere anticipation of Snapchat, just a click away, gives her an immediate and effortless spurt of dopamine. And because of the way this brain chemical works, once she clicks to chat, she'll want more.[7]

Dopamine is an adrenergic brain chemical. In other words, it's in the adrenaline family; it acts like a stimulant. When your child thinks about a hot stimulus such as Snapchat, dopamine stimulates the reward centers of her brain and activates her to seek it. If she makes a habit of going on Snapchat at homework time, she'll condition herself to its attention-grabbing level of stimulation. She'll lose her patience for less-stimulating activities like answering review questions.

Is the answer to make homework assignments more stimulating, perhaps by using learning apps and games? In some situations, yes. Apps and games are effective at motivating a child to keep playing and learning. They incorporate multiple strategies—intermittent winning, surprises, fast-moving action, striking graphics, catchy music, and more—to keep bottom-up pathways activated and high levels of dopamine flooding the reward pathways of the brain.

Learning apps are especially helpful when an undermotivated student needs a boost, but more stimulation is not always better. If a stimulus is strong enough to compel your child's attention, on a repeated basis it's strong enough to condition her to need higher levels of stimulation.

The purpose of education is to prepare children for adulthood, and the most successful adults are *not* controlled by the hottest stimulus in the room. In the marshmallow study, success as adults came to those who could resist an immediate temptation. Long after your child has forgotten the answers to her review questions, she'll benefit from the mental exercise that strengthened her ability to control her own attention without a steady stream of compelling sensory stimulation.

ATTENTION AND BRAIN PLASTICITY IN CHILDREN

Neuroscientists have a saying: "As the neuron fires, the brain rewires." It means that when you perform a behavior repeatedly, over time, your brain actually changes itself structurally to support that habit. "Plasticity," as it's called, will occur in support of any habit—good or bad.

Plasticity occurs throughout life, a fact discovered only in the late twentieth century. However, the rate of plasticity your child has now outpaces, by far, the rate she'll have as an adult. This is the main reason why habits learned in childhood are hard to break, and why names, poems, and jingles you memorized as a child stay with you all your life.

Compared to your brain and mine, your child's brain changes itself rapidly in response to her habits of attention. Night after night, answering her review questions makes her top-down pathways stronger and stronger, building the brain she'll need for future success. On the flip side, if, night after night, Snapchat wins over homework, plasticity will work against her. The brain she's building will make it harder for her to succeed in life.

You can see plasticity in action during the magic years when your child surprises you—and amazes her grandparents—with how quickly she learns animal sounds, colors, and the alphabet. But her brain is still forming well into early adulthood. A National Institutes of Health study using brain-imaging techniques showed that young people's brains undergo a massive reorganization between ages twelve to twenty-five, which includes synaptic pruning. In other words, brain connections that aren't used very much wither, while pathways that are used flourish.[8]

From birth to about her mid-twenties, your child's habits shape her brain in profound and lasting ways. One of the most interesting follow-up studies conducted with the preschoolers in the marshmallow test occurred forty years later, when twenty-six of the original subjects underwent brain imaging. High delayers—the children who held out the longest for their marshmallows—showed greater activity in their prefrontal cortex, which is the seat of voluntary attention. Low delayers showed greater activity in bottom-up pathways associated with involuntary attention.[9]

As you'll learn in chapter 3, the prefrontal cortex is the growth tip of your child's brain. Childhood, with its accelerated rate of brain plasticity, is the time to build voluntary attention and strengthen top-down neural pathways that will last a lifetime.

In chapter 3, we'll look at how a child's brain matures, how children's brains differ, and how to take your child's age and individuality into account when you make decisions as a parent.

3

Your Child's Amazing Brain

The brain is wider than the sky.

—Emily Dickinson

The human brain is unfathomably interconnected and communicates with itself instantaneously in extraordinarily complex, mind-boggling ways. The average human brain contains 100 billion neurons, with approximately one thousand to ten thousand synapses per typical neuron.[1] How does the brain reach this level of complexity and wonder?

Brain development in an infant starts with sensory and motor regions—evolutionally older, posterior parts of the brain. As your baby grows, her brain development moves forward to the newer prefrontal lobe, responsible for thinking. Research shows that a major shift occurs from the brain's orienting network (the bottom-up pathways of involuntary attention) to the brain's executive network (the top-down pathways of voluntary attention) by the age of three to four years.[2] The first few years of life are an extremely formative time in a baby's brain, especially for early construction of top-down brain pathways.

Although a child's brain has reached 90 percent of its full size by age six, it's far from fully developed, and there are specific parts of the brain that have the furthest to go. It is the newest brain region, the prefrontal cortex, responsible for executive functioning—including voluntary attention and metacognition—that still has years of growth ahead. Your child's behavior will be marked by impulsiveness and inconsistency for quite some time to come.

THE IMMATURE PREFRONTAL CORTEX

> He can play *Pokémon* for hours, totally focused. But ten minutes into an English assignment, he's texting and goofing off. —Brett's mom

> Reading's OK, but if I need to know something, I can google it. So what's the big deal? Gaming online with my friends is how I get smarter. —Brett, age eleven

Brett's got a point, doesn't he? He can google just about anything he wants to know. And when he's online gaming, he's improving certain sensory, cognitive, and physical skills and forging bonds with his gaming buddies. But at age eleven, Brett is hardly in a position to decide on his own educational needs. Brett lacks the judgment of an adult who can foresee problems that Google can't solve. Plus, he lacks the awareness of his own lack of judgment.

Brett's eleven-year-old prefrontal cortex keeps him thinking concretely, with limited ability for comprehending the importance of what's outside his direct experience. Success in gaming is Brett's measure of how smart a person is. Appreciating the knowledge, perspective, and wisdom that an adult has gained over several decades of life is too abstract a concept for an eleven-year-old's immature prefrontal cortex to process.

Abstract thinking, by the way, is not the same as imagination. In fact, children use imagination to fill in the gaps until they reach their capacity for higher-order reasoning. The esteemed developmental psychologist Jean Piaget cites the example of a small child walking through a village who claims that the moon is following him. Until the child is old enough to grasp the science of why it appears that way, he holds the fantasy of a willful and watchful moon.

Even well-behaved kids with superior intelligence are limited by the maturity of their prefrontal cortex. Because they're advanced in other ways, we have unrealistic expectations of their ability to make prudent decisions. Educational psychologists call this "asynchronous development." For instance, a child with a large vocabulary may use a sophisticated word correctly but lack depth in the meaning it has for him. A child may nod as you explain how homework is his ticket to higher education and a fulfilling career. But his understanding is concrete and straightforward. Doing homework gets you off his back so he has more time to play *Pokémon*.

HOW THE PREFRONTAL CORTEX MATURES

Both genes and environment determine the rate of maturity of the prefrontal cortex. Executive functions develop at different rates in children, and these rates are far more variable than the rates at which children learn to walk and talk.

Although these rates are variable, we still measure children's average rates of development, so we have some sense of what to expect. For instance, according to baselines established by the National Center for Educational Statistics, 20 percent of kindergarteners lag behind in thinking and attention skills and 31 percent in social and emotional development. This means they don't meet minimal expectations for their age for behaviors that require impulse control such as listening, stopping themselves from bothering others, controlling their anger, or accepting "no" for an answer.[3]

All executive functions mature in some way at every age, but there is a sequence during the growing years in which clusters of new executive skills build on previously learned ones. The main stages of this sequence are inhibition, working memory, and the ability to shift perspectives (also called "set shifting").[4]

DEVELOPMENTAL STAGES OF EXECUTIVE FUNCTIONING			
Ages	Birth to 6 years	7 to 12 years	13 to 18 years
Stages	Inhibition	Working memory	Ability to shift perspective

Birth to Six Years Old

In the first six years of life, developmental tasks for executive functions center around *inhibition*. Young children are learning to control their impulses to cry, throw tantrums, demand attention, and resort to extremes to get what they want. They need to learn to use their words, even when they're angry. As her brain matures, your child is forming important connections between her prefrontal cortex (her thinking brain) and her limbic system (her emotional brain). Watch her closely the next time she's disappointed but tries to keep her composure. Like the children in the marshmallow test, she may talk or sing sweetly to soothe herself—melt-your-heart signs of her efforts to build a strong prefrontal cortex.

Seven to Twelve Years Old

As tasks of inhibition continue, at around seven years, a child reaches what some call "the age of reason." Developmental tasks for executive functions now center around *working memory,* which allows your child to appreciate connections between cause and effect. From the time you held her in your arms, your child made immediate cause-and-effect connections, like flipping on a light switch. But now, she's able to reason things out. If the light doesn't turn on right away, is it plugged in? Does it need a new bulb? Are other lights still on? She can solve problems, applying information from her experience in new ways. This means she's able to anticipate the consequences of her actions over time, which greatly improves her ability to make decisions about her own behavior (even if she still starts the assignment she's had for weeks the night before it's due).

Thirteen to Eighteen Years Old

Throughout her teens, your child continues to improve inhibition and working memory. Now, however, developmental tasks for executive functions center around *the ability to shift perspectives* or move fluidly from one way of looking at things to another: concrete to abstract, micro to macro, present moment to the eternal, my world to yours. Until now, your child has been developing cognitive agility in many concrete situations, such as conversing at the table while texting under it. In adolescence, she can shift from current behavior to self-observation—from doing to seeing what she's doing through the eyes of others. She can now shift fluidly from under-the-table texting to what it looks like to you from across the table. Your teen is developing flexibility in abstract reasoning. She's now equipped for effective metacognition—thinking about her own thinking.

Nineteen to Twenty-Five Years Old

At eighteen years old, in the eyes of the law, your adult child has reached the age of majority (is no longer a minor) and assumes responsibility for herself. How ready is her brain for this? Although legally she's an adult, she can't rent a car without extra charges until she's twenty-five years of age. That's because rental car companies base their rates on actuarial statistics. After age twenty-five, the per-driver crash rate declines precipitously. Many years after these rates were established, brain-imaging studies revealed that the prefrontal cortex does not fully develop until at least the mid-twenties. In the words of researchers at MIT, "The rental car companies have it right."[5]

BRAIN AND BEHAVIOR WORKING TOGETHER

Does the development of the prefrontal cortex strengthen voluntary attention or do acts of voluntary attention develop the prefrontal cortex? The short answer to this chicken-or-egg question is: yes. The development of the prefrontal cortex strengthens voluntary attention *and* voluntary attention develops the prefrontal cortex.

It's useful to keep the sequence of this development in mind. You can then appreciate the big-picture value of situations such as helping your small child tolerate moderate frustration when she doesn't get what she wants right away. Her developmental task is to build inhibition. As we discussed in chapter 1, as a result of the marshmallow test, Mischel recommended that parents establish rules and rituals to help young children outsmart their immediate desires. An example of this is to routinely follow through when it's time to turn off the TV or touchcreen. If your child feels disappointed or upset or impatient, it's understandable to want to give in. But take a step back and see the added dimension of brain development—what's at stake and what your child can gain. A better but tougher choice is to listen and validate your child's feelings, then guide her to exercise self-control.

Another example is to encourage your grade-schooler to apply herself when homework gets hard. No one wants to watch a child struggle, but her developmental task is to strengthen her working memory, and no one can do that for her. Although you feel like rescuing your young student, instead you could suggest a short break and root for her to rise to the occasion. "I know that you're frustrated with this assignment. How about we listen to that new song you like and come back to this? I know you can do it."

Understanding how executive functions develop can help you have realistic expectations and not take matters personally when your child acts as though her brain isn't fully functional. (It's not.)

You'll learn specific ways to put these ideas into action in Step Five (chapter 8).

SOME FACTS ABOUT DEVELOPMENTAL DELAYS

The use of developmental milestones can be tricky. Since children mature at such different rates, it's unfair to compare one child to another, especially siblings at the same age. Yet, while variation in development is to be expected, parents need to know when a child is falling behind and it's time to get him some extra help.

Because the prefrontal cortex is where a child's brain shows the most growth, the largest differences in rates of neuro-development in children are in their executive functions, especially their voluntary attention. This causes problems for late bloomers. For example, when students go from having one teacher in one classroom in elementary school to having multiple teachers and changing classes in middle school, some children are ready and some are not. If their struggles to stay focused and organized in school go unrecognized, they'll start to lag. They get discouraged, lose interest, and distract themselves to feel better, which worsens matters at school.

If your child has developmental delays in executive functioning, get him the help he needs as quickly as possible, before he decides he's a failure—but don't jump to conclusions about what this means for the rest of his life. Important new research suggests that more often than not, symptoms of inattention, impulsivity, and hyperactivity decrease with age. A Columbia University study identified fifteen hundred children who had been assessed and diagnosed with ADHD. Within two years, over 50 percent of the children had lost their diagnosis. In other words, the severity of their symptoms no longer met the criteria for this disorder.[6]

According to the National Institutes of Health, the brains of children who have ADHD mature in a normal pattern but are delayed an average of three years in certain regions of the prefrontal cortex. Previous brain-imaging studies failed to detect this developmental lag but a new imaging-analysis technique allowed researchers to identify it.[7]

As we discussed in chapter 1, the brain alters itself in response to learning. In *The Brain That Changes Itself*, psychiatrist Norman Doidge points out that while scientists have, for several decades now, embraced the reality of brain plasticity, on a wider scale, it's taking some time to overturn centuries of belief that structural change in the brain is impossible.[8] Doidge reminds us that the model of the brain as a "hardwired" machine is an outdated, faulty analogy that undercuts human potential. Machines don't grow new parts. The brain grows organically in response to behavior that's repeated. Brain pathways are more like waterways or tree roots, which create their own paths as they grow.

Calling the brain "hardwired" has been particularly unhelpful in discussions about attention deficit disorder. Evidence of brain plasticity, especially in childhood, together with findings on how long it takes for the prefrontal cortex to mature, makes the outcome of childhood ADHD an open-ended question.

Most definitely, children are born with genetic predispositions that influence how their brains develop. Some children have strong innate tendencies for ADHD, but environmental factors matter, too. Research overwhelmingly supports the fact that ADHD is a heterogeneous disorder. In other words, it encompasses a continuum of disorders that have different clusters of symptoms and multiple causes.[9]

While many adults have ADHD, a child with ADHD will not necessarily be impaired as an adult. A longitudinal study published in 2013 used brain imaging to track children with ADHD into their mid-twenties. In 40 percent of the children, the disorder persisted and results showed cortical thinning in networks that support voluntary attention. In the 60 percent for whom the disorder had remitted, results showed cortical thickening or minimal thinning in those same areas.[10]

Although it's harder for children with ADHD to do so, they need to practice voluntary attention and build top-down brain pathways in order to improve. The challenge is to stay focused on your child's abilities and strengths, so he feels motivated to shore up his weaknesses.

If your child is showing symptoms of an attention disorder, have him assessed. Stop the cycle of failure by providing understanding and support—accommodations with homework and deadlines, special resources to help him stay organized and on track, and a medication evaluation if necessary. But keep in mind that for the best possible outcome, he needs to exercise voluntary attention on a regular basis, even though it's harder on you and him than it is when ADHD is not in the picture.

NEURODIVERSITY

> Looking back now, I realize I had no reason to expect Noah to behave the way Collin did at his age, but at the time, I was stunned. Collin used to turn off his Xbox when I asked him to, but Noah keeps playing. I'll stand there, inches from his nose, and he keeps playing, as if I don't exist. —Noah's dad

We have different faces and different fingerprints, yet often, we forget how different our brain chemistries can be—what scientists call "neurodiversity." The interaction of different brain chemicals with each other and with the environment plays a critical role in differences among children, such as Noah's hyperfocus and determination to play his Xbox and his brother's open focus and accessibility while playing.

Neurodiversity underlies the fact that each child has a unique set of cognitive strengths and weaknesses, and matures at his own pace and in his own way. For a parent, this means getting to know and appreciate each of your children as an individual and discovering that what works with one child may not work with another. For example, Noah needs a lot more structure to his Xbox time than Collin did, including schedules and signals ahead of time to prepare him to transition from virtual to real world. As he gets older, he'll need to set rules for himself and stay keenly self-aware of his propensity to undermine them.

How do you deal with outcries of "It's not fair!" from siblings, or more important, from yourself? Shouldn't parents treat every child the same? Living under the same roof, each member of your family sees the same things, including the way that each of your children responds differently to the same thing. Deep down, you know, and they know, that as long as you're fair and don't play favorites, the best thing to do is to treat them the same by treating them differently.

THE NOVELTY GENE

Scientists have sought to link genes with brain chemicals but have found, not surprisingly, that predicting human behavior is a lot more complicated than predicting eye color. Typically, in genetic studies of executive functions including voluntary attention, effects are small and difficult to replicate, involve multiple systems, and appear to influence some processes but not others.[11]

One line of research, relevant to the development of attention problems, is the study of genetic variants of the brain chemical dopamine. One type and form, in particular, appears to play a role in how strongly a person is attracted to newness and change.[12] It's been nicknamed the "novelty gene," although no single gene corresponds to a single kind of behavior.

An estimated 20 percent of people carry this gene, which predisposes them to invest less mental energy in weighing realistic outcomes and more in the anticipation of the next new thing. In other words, they tend to seek stimulation and have a low tolerance for boredom—characteristics that make them prime targets for attention snatchers.

A review of twenty-one studies of this type of gene (called DRD4-7R) documented a significant association with attention deficit disorder.[13] While having the gene may put a child at risk for ADHD, clearly not everyone with DRD4-7R develops the disorder. Plus, a genetic predisposition for being spurred to action can be a good thing. In fact, genetic studies at the University of California at Irvine showed a positive selection for DRD4-7R, linking it to successful migration cultures.[14]

Imagine that a tribe of our ancestors lived in a settlement by a river but had a tough winter and were out of food. To ensure survival, some would have to travel up the river to start a new settlement. Those who were genetically most inclined to crave new experience went. Their brain chemistry favored adventure and discovery. Years later, if the new settlement faced harsh conditions, once again, the most dopamine-driven among them led the way farther into uncharted territory.

In situations like these, our species needs individuals who can act first and think later. We need members who are capable of reduced consideration for long-term consequences.[15] In a 2013 *National Geographic* article, DRD4-7R was dubbed the "explorer gene."[16]

The *National Geographic* article described how African tribesmen who carry the gene were stronger in nomadic tribes and weaker in settled ones. Their restless behavior in settlements resembled what we call ADHD today. When I read this, I was reminded of the way kids with ADHD have been called hunters in a farmer's world.[17]

ADHD symptoms, such as a short attention span, poor planning, and impulsivity, can also be viewed as "hunter" traits—constantly monitoring the environment, being ready for the chase, and having a willingness to risk. These hunter traits conflict with classroom ideals, which reward "farmer" traits—maintaining concentration, sticking to a plan, and acting with care.

Perspectives like these can motivate children with ADHD to cooperate. For instance, kids with ADHD are tired of being told they're doing something wrong. They'll try harder to slow down and check their work if we acknowledge their "hunter" ability to get it done fast as a potential strength and then tell them that it's time to learn a "farmer" skill, as well.

THE EDISON TRAIT

In 1997, also before the genetic studies on the positive selection of DRD4-7R, I wrote about the approximately 20 percent of the population who favored "divergent thinking." Divergent thinkers are attracted to new, stimulating, and often impractical ideas, the more original, the better. Because those who are prone to think divergently don't automatically censor ideas that everyone else does, they tend to be visionaries, innovators, and entrepreneurs. As kids, they are dreamers, discoverers, and dynamos. Their profile was called the "Edison trait," for the prolific inventor Thomas Edison.

My first book, *Dreamers, Discoverers, and Dynamos: How to Help the Child Who Is Bright, Bored, and Having Problems in School,*[18] was written for parents of Edison-trait children. These nonconforming kids need to learn to follow rules and build their voluntary attention without losing their creativity and spontaneity. Most likely at least one of them has already thought up the next revolutionary app, but it will become a reality only if he can stay focused long enough to make it happen.

When I wrote the book, divergent thinkers made up a large part of my practice and also the practices of many of my colleagues. Divergent-thinking kids struggle because schools require "convergent thinking" —that is, the ability to stay on task and resist distracting thoughts and irrelevant stimulation. Some of these divergent thinkers were diagnosed with ADHD but many were not. Prevalence for the disorder averaged 4 percent at that time but has steadily increased since then to 11 percent, or 6.4 million children in 2011.[19]

THE POWER OF BRAIN PLASTICITY

In today's world, with attention snatchers in every home, the brain chemistry of every child is at greater risk for problems with attention than it has ever been in the past. Because of brain plasticity, as children engage in habits that weaken voluntary attention, their brains grow to support those habits.

But the reverse is true, as well. Because of brain plasticity, as children engage in habits that strengthen voluntary attention, their brains grow to support those healthier habits. If your child is currently overusing her electronics, don't be discouraged. Her executive functions are a work in progress.

In *The Power of Habit*, the journalist Charles Duhigg looks at the impact of brain plasticity and how the repetition of small, new behaviors eventually change lives. The most powerful habit of all, he concludes, is the habit of believing in change.[20]

Coming up in part two are the seven steps to build your child's voluntary attention. In chapter 4, we'll look at the first step: "Get Into the Right Mind-set." Kids have a radar for knowing when parents say one thing but think another. That's why we begin the seven steps with *your* awareness and attitude.

PART TWO

Seven Steps to Teach Your Child to Pay Attention

Step One
Get Into the Right Mind-set

Step Two
Be the Change You Want to See in Your Child

Step Three
Practice the 3 Rs of Good Attention

Step Four
Turn Up Real-World Happiness

Step Five
Think Like a Child, Act Like a Parent

Step Six
Become a Focus-Friendly Family

Step Seven
Celebrate Success but Prepare for Stronger Snatchers

4

Step One
Get Into the Right Mind-set

Nothing can stop the man with the right mental attitude from achieving his goal; nothing on earth can help the man with the wrong mental attitude.

—Thomas Jefferson

In part one, we saw that the single factor most predictive of your child's success is his ability to allocate his own attention. We discussed two types of attention, voluntary and involuntary, and how attention snatchers capture children's involuntary attention, which can leave their voluntary attention weak.

We also looked at how your child's brain is still developing, particularly the pathways down from the prefrontal cortex, and why your child needs to practice voluntary attention for this brain growth to occur.

In part two, you'll learn the seven steps to help your child build voluntary attention. The first step starts with you—your view of your child's attention and your role in shaping it.

LEARN TO DISTINGUISH BETWEEN VOLUNTARY AND INVOLUNTARY ATTENTION

Let's say your twelve-year-old is a pretty good student but this year school is getting harder. Lately, his mind has been wandering in classes that he doesn't like. Also, he's been getting more disorganized and having trouble settling down when class is about to begin. He's a good kid, has a smartphone, knows his way around the Internet, likes to watch sports on TV, is skilled at video games, and is crazy about anything that has to do with aviation.

Having recently received e-mails from your son's teachers about his distractability, you've started talking with him about it. Today, when he came home from school, he told you that he learned about Charles Lindbergh's flight from New York to Paris and that this class was so interesting, he paid total attention the whole time. His teacher even complimented him on it.

What do you say?

a. "That's great. I'm glad you got to learn about that and also that Mr. Wilson noticed you were paying attention."
b. "If only you had the same kind of attention when it comes to history lessons that have nothing to do with planes."
c. "What do you suppose is the difference between how you paid attention today and paying attention when the lesson isn't about flying?"
d. All of the above
e. (a) and (c) but not (b)

Looking through the lens of "Is it voluntary or involuntary attention?" here's what we know about this student:

This young man has spent enough time on digital devices to be accustomed to the experience of involuntary attention. He's come to expect that paying attention is easy, because it happens effortlessly in those circumstances. In earlier grades, he could slide by. But now he needs to exercise effortful attention at school and doesn't quite know how.

He's weak in voluntary attention, which he needs for tasks that have low stimulation—classroom lessons that don't entertain him, the dull job of putting papers in their proper places, and transitions from the freedom and fun of the hallways to the silent focus of the classsroom. With no external cues from a screen, he has to make a real effort to control his attention—a very different kind of experience for him.

A parent looking through the lens of "voluntary or involuntary attention?" would recognize that her aviation-minded son's attention to a lesson on Lindbergh didn't require much effort and so it doesn't indicate that his voluntary attention is getting stronger.

Now let's consider the answers:

> Answer (a) is positive and helps build this young man's motivation. Also, it's worded in a way that doesn't imply that his attentiveness to today's lesson necessarily shows he's improving his voluntary attention.
>
> Answer (b) has truth to it, but it's deflating, confusing, and could hurt the child's feelings. You certainly want your child to have a realistic expectation that history lessons that don't involve planes require something different from him than those that do—namely, sustained effort to pay attention. But it's best to come at it with kindness and compassion.
>
> Answer (c) is the prelude to an important conversation about the difference between attention that's captured and attention that requires effort. Your child needs to understand and accept that not all attention is the same. In fact, changing that expectation is at the core of what he needs to do. Think of the difference in your experience between going to a movie versus taking your receipts out to prepare your taxes. If you expect that attention is going to come as easily to you at your desk as it does in the theater, you'll still be waiting to be entertained by your 1040 form long past April fifteenth.
>
> Your child has presented you with a teachable moment, and answer (c) is a good lead into it. If you've preceded this conversation

with answer (a), celebrating his enthusiasm about today's lesson with him, he'll be more open to hearing what you have to say. So, to both motivate your child and help him establish realistic expectations about voluntary attention, answer (e) is your best bet.

By the way, this example is a scenario that plays out in a majority of cases in my practice these days. Most of the children I see innocently expect to have their attention captured. They don't get that it's up to them to pay attention to a lesson or a task that doesn't pull them in. We've conditioned their brains to expect a compelling external source of stimulation. As far as they're concerned, attention should require little or no effort on their part. They're not spoiled or entitled. They're accustomed to involuntary attention and unfamiliar with the effort they need for voluntary attention.

PRACTICE USING THE LENS OF "VOLUNTARY OR INVOLUNTARY ATTENTION?"

As we saw in chapter 2, *voluntary attention* is effortful and a result of your own decision. In contrast, *involuntary attention* is effortless, a reaction to an external stimulus or cue.

The first step to helping your children build strong voluntary attention skills is to become aware of the difference between voluntary and involuntary attention in the course of their day. When you see your child doing homework, think "voluntary attention." When you see her watching a video, think "involuntary attention."

Intuitively, we sense this difference. It fits with our own everyday experience. Let's say you came home from work exhausted, got dinner on the table, helped the kids with homework, and did a few chores. You could sit at your desk and take care of some paperwork, but you don't have the attention for it. Instead, you sit down and turn the TV on. Hours later, you wonder where the time has gone. You didn't have the attention for your desk work, but you did have the attention to watch several TV shows. Your inner experience tells you that something *feels* different about attention for work and attention to the TV. And sure enough, what's happening inside your brain is different—very different.

Your tasks at work and home were effortful acts of voluntary attention, originating in your prefrontal cortex. The hours of TV were effortless acts of involuntary attention, originating in your sensory cortex.

When you look through a lens that filters for voluntary or involuntary attention, you can see that by the time you sat down to watch TV, you had exerted mental effort all day and all evening, and you felt like your brain was fried. But that wasn't entirely true. Your prefrontal cortex was fried. Your sensory cortex was ready to be entertained, especially now that your pesky prefrontal cortex—seat of executive functions, such as good judgment and time management—was out of commission to decide against it.

Let's use this lens to look at your children's day. During classtime, they exercised voluntary attention. When they came home, if they're like most children, they engaged in digital media, using mostly involuntary attention. According to a 2010 survey by the Kaiser Family Foundation, children ages eight to eighteen spend over fifty-three hours per week—an average of seven hours and thirty-eight minutes per day—on entertainment media. According to the report, when you account for multitasking—for example, texting and watching TV—they average eleven hours per day.[1] When children start their homework (occasionally checking Instagram and Twitter) they'll exercise mostly voluntary attention.

Naming attention as voluntary or involuntary fosters awareness. When you routinely ask the question, "Is it voluntary or involuntary attention?" you'll see how well attention snatchers do their job. Use this lens the same way that you mentally label what's nutritious and non-nutritious, or high- or low-calorie, when you look at what your kids eat. Just as most dishes have both highly nourishing and not-so-nourishing ingredients, you'll find that for most activities, your child uses both voluntary and involuntary attention.

For example, educational apps use compelling sights and sounds that engage your child's involuntary attention and also recruit some voluntary attention. That makes them useful to get kids to spend more time with subjects they don't like, much the same way we get kids to eat veggies by adding tasty sauces.

A good time to practice on yourself is when you're on social media. See what happens when you keep asking the question, "Is this mostly voluntary or mostly involuntary attention?" You begin with a goal—to catch up with friends—but then what you see onscreen takes over. You find yourself clicking on cute cat videos or vines with teasers like "Unbelievable. Will instantly make you feel happy." Notice this shift as quickly as you can, once it starts to happen.

You want your children to have this kind of awareness by the time they reach adulthood, but for now, you'll need to have this awareness for them. As you observe your kids' attention through this lens, try not to get judgmental, critical, worried, discouraged, or defensive. As much as possible, take a step back and be an objective observer. Keep in mind that no matter what you see through this lens, change is possible. Your child's brain is still very much under construction.

Awareness alone leads to better choices. The more you use this lens to observe your children, the more you'll find yourself thinking up enjoyable activities of voluntary attention, the way you think up recipes to get them to like eating greens.

Seeing through this new lens makes the invisible visible, so you can take action before visible problems arise. But don't let this new vision lead you to shame your child, become rigid, or nag. (Not as easy as it sounds, but more on this later in the chapter.) As your children get older, you'll have fewer opportunities to directly observe them. If your rules are too strict, or if they feel you're down on them for too much screentime, they'll make a show of voluntary attention at home and let attention snatchers have their way when you're not around. Observe without blame. You're laying the groundwork for them to *want* to self-observe.

Ask yourself, "What kind of attention is my child exercising right now?" Do it often, so it becomes a strong habit. *Does this activity require mostly voluntary or involuntary attention?* Soon it will be second nature, the way you know the nutritional value of an apple or a french fry.

EXPECT RESISTANCE TO VOLUNTARY ATTENTION

As you strengthen your habit of discriminating voluntary from involuntary attention, you'll notice an instant giveaway as to how much voluntary attention a task requires. It's the relative ease of your child's transition in and out of it. If she resists getting started—for instance, doing her homework—the task requires voluntary attention. If she resists stopping—for instance, watching videos—it's an involuntary attention snatcher.

As you learned in chapter 2, involuntary attention is the path of least resistance. On the flip side, voluntary attention is the path of most resistance. By definition, voluntary attention requires effort. Your child must overcome inertia to shift from watching videos to concentrating on her homework.

You may wonder, "What good is it to expect resistance, if it's going to happen anyway?" The value is that when you know what to expect, you aren't ambushed by the unexpected. You can prepare for it, mentally, emotionally, and logistically.

To appreciate the benefits of expecting resistance, imagine that it's time for your child to turn off her 3DS and begin an assignment for school.

First, if you see resistance coming, you can stay calm, think clearly, and more effectively help your child overcome it. You can keep the big picture in mind. Getting started is the hardest part, but once your child dives in, she'll get into the swim of things. Anticipating your child's resistance prevents you from unintentionally getting caught up in it, too. You can keep a tone of quiet confidence that she can and will succeed.

Second, when you see resistance for what it is—a naturally occurring phenomenon—you can separate the resistance from the resister. You're less likely to take your child's lack of compliance personally and more likely to provide age-appropriate structure and creative strategies for her to jump in and get started.

Third, you can plan for it logistically:

- Allow for the amount of time and freedom from distraction that your child needs to get started.
- Allocate enough of your own time and attention to support her efforts in a positive way.
- Adjust the family schedule so there are no additional demands on her or you.

Eventually, with structure and support and no battle scenes, as your child matures, she'll learn to recognize and overcome resistance on her own.

Think of the word PLAN:

P is for Project. Anticipate your child's resistance by projecting into the future.
L is for Logistics. Allocate time, adult supervision, and other practical considerations.
A is for Action. Follow through, even when *you* feel resistance.
N is for No Drama. Stay calm and don't take the bait. Arguments create diversions and homework still doesn't get done.

> We had a nice family evening planned—dinner and a movie. He had about twenty minutes of homework to do. But he dawdled with fantasy sports online, even though he wasn't supposed to. We can't take away the tablet when he needs it for an assignment. So, everybody got mad, and we wound up canceling the night. —Todd's mom

How can expecting Todd's resistance help this parent next time? For starters, having learned from this frustrating evening, most likely not the only one of its kind, our hero, Todd's mom, will not, for the time being, schedule a family night again when Todd has homework of any length. That will reduce the pressure. It won't always have to be this way. After Todd's homework habits improve, Todd's mom can gauge which nights he needs this kind of consideration and which nights he'll be OK. Meanwhile, the family can still go out on the spur of the moment if Todd finishes early enough.

Next, Todd's mom will consider the least intrusive but most effective supervisory strategy. For example, she could bring her own work into the same room as Todd, staying focused on her tasks, not his, and remembering to turn off her smartphone. Some kids respond well to this, while others can't leave a parent alone if she's sitting right there. You'll learn more strategies throughout the rest of this book, but what matters here is that, by anticipating her son's resistance, Todd's mom can prepare herself to use firm, fair, patient persistence to help her son get going.

> Her paper has been due for weeks. She sits at the computer to write it, but when she starts to do research on the Internet, she changes her mind about the topic or the approach or even if she should be taking this class at all. Then she spends the night online looking at college majors and career possibilities.
> —Sarah's mom

With the right mind-set, Sarah's mom will recognize her daughter's resistance to getting started and refrain from engaging in a discussion about her future, which would only prolong her daughter's avoidance of writing the paper and reinforce her endless diversion of online searching.

This may be a hard thing for Sarah's mom to do, assuming that, like most offspring, Sarah has subconsciously learned to assure successful avoidance by pushing her mother's hot buttons—the specific one this evening being her fear for her daughter's future. Having prepared herself for this moment, Sarah's mom punts: "Let's talk about that on Saturday."

Sarah's mom then introduces some age-appropriate structure, such as, "What's your time frame for finishing an outline on this paper?" She jots it down, along with a happy face, and leaves it on Sarah's desk. She's also prepared to follow up with some quick, pleasant drop-in visits to shower her daughter with recognition for any real work accomplished and to notice, without judgment or criticism, her progress on the timeline. Again, the remaining chapters of this book will have more ideas for specific strategies, but they all start with a calm, can-do mind-set that accepts resistance to effortful attention as a fact of life.

There's nothing new under the sun about procrastination, particularly for kids. Or is there? As children, you and I had immature executive functions, just as our children do today. The parts of our brains responsible for voluntary attention weren't fully developed either. But for the first time, children today, with immature executive functions and still-developing brains, must contend with attention snatchers that are ubiquitous and compelling. And so, for the first time, parents need a mind-set that effectively protects kids from attention snatching and teaches them the skills they need to protect themselves, as well.

EXPECT A DESIRE TO QUIT WHEN IT GETS HARD

As you strengthen your habit of discriminating your child's voluntary from involuntary attention, you'll notice yet another instant giveaway. As a task gets more difficult, so will your child. You'll notice avoidance, diversionary tactics, or a statement of protest: "It's too hard." Wanting to quit when greater effort is required is another sign of resistance to voluntary attention.

Video games and educational apps are engineered to provide ample stimuli to draw a child into the challenge of playing at the next level. This is a real plus to get a child to learn the particular skills of that game. But at the same time, it accustoms a child to be pulled into facing a more difficult challenge by high levels of sensory stimulation. In real life, she needs to step up to the plate of her own accord.

> Doug's so bright that he's never had to study for tests. Now, in the fourth grade, he needs to, and he just shuts down. I know he's afraid of failure, but nothing seems to help. —Doug's dad

Fearing failure for his son, Doug's dad spent a small fortune on educational software to reengage Doug in schoolwork. To some extent, this strategy worked. He was tempted to buy even more but he understood that his son needed the ability to sustain his attention without the software, too. Doug's dad is hiring a ninth-grader to come by twice a week to help Doug learn how to study and prepare for tests.

> Trish does this with every sport she's tried. She starts out happy to be out there with her friends, but when she gets to a level of play on the field where she has to concentrate, she loses interest and she's back to playing games online. —Trish's dad

Understandably, Trish's dad is frustrated. He can see that his daughter enjoys sports and that she wants to improve. Also, he realizes the importance of his daughter learning to follow through when the going gets tough. But he's in a better place to help his daughter when he shifts his mind-set to expect, without blame, her resistance to focus when it gets hard for her. He can help prepare her *before* she wants to quit. He can say, "Let's be ready for when you don't feel like sticking with it. Go on. If you were a coach, what would you say to yourself when that happens?" He can have Trish write down her own messages to her future self: "I can do it." "Keep going." "I will do this and feel proud!" and then save them to give to her when she feels like giving up.

STAY CALM

There's one more critical difference between voluntary and involuntary attention, and it's related to the way dopamine, a stimulating brain chemical, is being metabolized. When your child engages in voluntary attention, his brain—specifically his prefrontal cortex—prevents extremes of emotion, so his feelings don't take over.[2] As he filters information, he stays on an even keel and strengthens the executive function of emotional self-regulation.

When your child is engaged in involuntary attention, older parts of the brain are in play that do not modulate emotion but rather intensify the fight-or-flight response. Your child's brain is hampered in its ability to regulate emotional pressure. Extremes of emotion take but a hair trigger to discharge. This could help explain David Pogue's account in chapter 1 of his son getting "bizarrely upset . . . out-of-character upset" when he's told to turn off his iPad. Many parents have told me that, like Pogue, they've been surprised by their child's extreme reactions when having to turn off their devices.

The link between involuntary attention and a loss of the ability to regulate emotional pressure is no small matter. Cyberbullying, bashing, flaming (posting hostile insults), and online rudeness are believed to be the result of anonymity on the Internet, and they are, to a large degree. But hotheaded behavior online is also due to the fact that, without voluntary attention, the part of the brain that regulates emotional reactivity is not working at full strength. Think of what happens if your water-pressure regulator falters and water from the street roars into your house. You can expect a broken pipe or two.

When it's time for your child to hit the off button on his digital device, what he says or does may provoke you. Don't lose your temper (which is easier said than done). Keep in mind that his prolonged involuntary attention has led him to emotional extremes and use this knowledge to prevent further escalation at this point.

If your child behaves disrespectfully, calmly hold him accountable. He needs a clear, constructive message that disrepect is unacceptable. This is crucial for him to own responsibility for his own behavior. Use his transgression as a teachable moment, to calmly require him to apologize, make reparation if he acted offensively, and come up with a plan and a promise not to do it again. If he's so emotionally out of control that his thinking brain is temporarily inaccessible, wait until he's calm and then hold him accountable. If it's a repeated offense, consider the connection between overuse of screentime and loss of emotional control, and set limits accordingly. But don't take his defiance personally.

Here's one of my favorite images for a model parenting style that reduces the intensity of emotional reactivity. It can also prevent resentment and the futile habit of nagging.

Imagine that you've been speeding, and a police officer pulls you over. He doesn't scream, "I saw you. Don't you dare tell me you weren't doing it." He doesn't sob, "I can't believe you're doing this again." And he doesn't lecture you until you're half asleep.

A good police officer pulls you over, gives you his undivided attention, and treats you with respect. He clearly identifies what you did wrong and holds you accountable for it.

When children need to be corrected, the police-officer style of parenting can keep *our* emotions self-regulated, even when our children's emotions are not. Also, while it's understandable to feel angry, strive to be a kind police officer, especially for young children.

BE ON THE SAME SIDE

When you remind your child that it's time to put away his electronics, momentarily, you are the enemy. He has an immature brain that's been captured by a screen. All the while he's been in a state of involuntary attention, pressure has been building up inside him. Now his emotional brain wants what it wants.

You need to guide him because his ability to turn from activities of involuntary attention to activities of voluntary attention, without drama, is critical to his future. The effort you make to follow through with him now will pay off for years to come. He'll have greater personal self-control so there'll be fewer emotionally charged conflicts between you.

If you feel exasperated and hear yourself saying, "I can't fight this battle, too," take a deep breath and shift perspective. Just because he sees you as the enemy, you don't have to accept that role. You and your child want the same things—his future success in school and in life, building the healthiest, strongest brain possible, having a good time living under the same roof, and being a happy family. You're on the same side. You're allies, not enemies. Refuse to accept the image of a battle.

You may need to be police-officer serious to correct him, but you don't have to be on opposites sides. Take a step back and see a bigger picture. Many TV comedies about parents and children rely on how humorous a control battle appears to an outside observer. Everyone except the arguers can see how futile they are.

Use metacognition and ask yourself the question, "What am I *not* thinking of now?" Look to your heart and refuse to see a dividing wall. See a bridge, instead.

STAY MOTIVATED

In a world of technology and distraction, the job of helping your child build voluntary attention is a lonely one with delayed rewards. You invest time and effort now for your child's success in the future—a challenging, years-long marshmallow test for parents.

Guard against a "poor me" mentality, especially when you're tired or frustrated. Catch yourself, so you don't dwell on unhelpful thoughts—for instance, "I've had it. I just can't do one more thing." Use metacognition: "What am I *not* thinking about?" Change gears as quickly as you can. Sometimes, self-talk can help.

- Be a hero, not a victim: *I'm enriching our lives, not restricting them.*
- Keep an attitude of gratitude: *I'm grateful to be a parent through good times and bad.*
- Eyes on the prize: *My child and I are investing in his future.*

It will always be easier to give in than to redirect your child, but *it will get easier, the more you do it*. Inevitably, there will be slumps in your motivation. Reflect on how you've succeeded in life and what it took for you to get there. Keep the dots connected between building your child's voluntary attention now and his success and happiness in the future.

We want our children to achieve in school, and often the reason we don't have time to get them off their iPads is because we're working our tails off to save money for their college tuitions. Remind yourself that without the ability to control his own attention, your child won't get into a good college even if you've saved the money to pay for it. When you're emotionally exhausted and wondering if your efforts are worth it, keep a mental picture of your child as a college graduate and a successful, self-reliant adult.

USE FORESIGHT AND STAND YOUR GROUND

Have the courage of your convictions, even if you have to swim against the current. Our existing cultural message is that playing with electronics should be a child's preferred activity.

> Teacher: "If you can't behave yourself when we're at the computers, you'll have to get a book and learn today's lesson that way." This seems like a natural consequence for a student who's messing around at computer time and it's not at all uncommon. But what are students hearing? *Computers are cool. Books are not.*

> Mom: "Finish writing out the story and you can play on your iPad." Children are naturals at storytelling. But what is this little girl learning? *Writing is drudgery; playing on my iPad is fun.*

Uniformly, the advice to parents on raising kids in the digital age is to be involved. But it's essential to be involved in the right way. What if this mom chose a different angle to help motivate her daughter—an approach that didn't make playing on her iPad such a sought-after reward? Instead, what if she linked her child's story-writing to the good feelings she'll have about herself and the recognition she'll get for it at school?

She might say, "Writing a story is playing make-believe with words," or "Once you get started, you may not want to stop!" or "I can hardly wait to see what you write! Are you going to draw pictures, too?" or

"When you're done, we can send it to Grandma. She loves to read your stories." And when the little girl has finished, her mom can remind her, "You can feel mighty proud of yourself. Wait 'til Ms. Martin sees this. You put your mind to it and it shows."

Consistently using digital media as a reward for your child, or forbidding it as a punishment, is a recipe for disaster. When you're not around, in person, to catch your child's hand in the cookie jar, she'll eat every last crumb. She'll indulge in digital media every chance she can at the cost of her own best interest.

If you look around a college dorm at night, you'll see some kids diligently studying and some who are drunk on freedom, their screens aglow with social media or action games until dawn. Which ones, do you think, connected the dots between effortful attention and future rewards for their efforts, and which ones couldn't wait to break rules they didn't buy into—but might have, if digital media hadn't been such a dangling carrot for them?

In the long run, the only strategy that works is for your child to grow up wanting to limit her own use of digital media, so she's motivated to exercise her voluntary attention even when nobody else is looking. For this to happen, she needs to internalize this value, which starts with you and the subtle (and not-so-subtle) messages you send about which activities are desirable and which are not.

The technology industry has a pretty big stake in recruiting children while they're young to choose technology above all else. We tend to perpetuate that bias, unaware that we're doing it. But we don't have to buy into their marketing strategy or our own peer pressure to appear techno-cool. Let's look with our own eyes and stand up for the merits of activities that foster voluntary attention, even if it means going against the crowd.

In chapter 3, you read about the developmental stages in children. When it's time to get a toddler off an iPad, kindly, yet firmly, redirect her. Guide a school-age child using concrete terms, connecting homework and studying with good grades. For an older child, use broader concepts such as plans for college. You'll learn more strategies for each stage of development in Step Five (chapter 8). For now, keep in mind that when you ask yourself the metacognitive question, "What am I *not* thinking of?" the answer could be, "That my child's brain is not fully grown."

In the next chapter, "Step Two: Be the Change You Want to See in Your Child," you'll learn how your actions are the most powerful messages you can give your children about their consumption of digital media.

5

Step Two
Be the Change You Want to See in Your Child

Children grow well when their
parents are growing well.
—W. D. Wall

Children do as we do, not as we say, but it's hard to be a good role model. When it comes to attention snatchers, we adults are not immune. We enjoy a good dopamine rush, and when we work long hours all day, our only links to excitement are URLs. We're forming habits of involuntary attention, too.

In one study, adults were instructed to pick a time at home when they didn't feel rushed. They were to refrain from using their electronic devices while sitting alone with their thoughts. They lasted from six to twelve minutes.[1] (In the marshmallow test, 30 percent of the four-year-olds held out fifteen minutes for their treats!)

BE AWARE OF THE MESSAGE YOUR ACTIONS SEND

The insightful psychiatrist Carl Jung once said, "If there is anything we wish to change in the child, we should first examine it and see whether it is not something that could better be changed in ourselves." When it comes to self-control and attention snatchers, Jung nailed it.

A bright, articulate second-grader had been referred to me, because despite the best efforts of her teacher, principal, and parents, she could not seem to pay attention to classroom instruction. She completed her assignments, but during class, when the teacher was talking, she'd start to do something else.

Being a child whose prefrontal cortex is still developing and who still answers questions in concrete terms, when asked why she did this, the little girl replied, "I don't know." She didn't meet the criteria for ADHD. The vice-principal suspected an auditory processing problem or possibly a nervous habit.

We started a behavioral program at school and got formal testing under way, but as I grew to know her parents better, I began to see a pattern in the family interactions. Her mom and dad had vowed to be present in their daughter's life. Their own upwardly mobile parents, especially their fathers, hadn't spent much time with them.

To accomplish this, both parents telecommuted from home, dividing their attention between their daughter and their computers. It wasn't easy on them, but they were committed. They didn't see the unintended consequences of this routine—how their ongoing divided attention played a role in their daughter's formative habits. When they did, they started to monitor their daily actions. They stopped giving their daughter partial attention, which meant a big change in their daily routines. They did their best to give their full attention to their child on a regular basis and attend to their jobs when they weren't with her. Although it took quite some time, their child began to pay more attention at school, too.

Theirs is not an isolated case. Many times, older children whose grades are suffering from too much multitasking tell me that their parents do it all the time. Parents will explain their need to check e-mails and texts for work, which is understandable. Nonetheless, greater awareness of how your habits impact your child can help you take steps to minimize harmful effects.

Make it the exception, not the rule. Reacting to a ringtone or onscreen alert causes a stimulant boost in our brains. We're drawn to it and we want more. Once we give ourselves permission to react automatically, our brain chemistry produces the urge to do it next time, too. Don't let this pattern take over. Give yourself intentional, reasonable rules: for example, answer only truly urgent business calls. Or, turn off your ringer, put your smartphone away, and leave the room to check for messages once every half hour or so. By doing this, you're flipping the habit from an automatic act of involuntary attention—your device telling you what to do and when to do it—to an effortful act of voluntary attention in which *you* decide when and where you'll attend to your device.

Excuse and remove yourself. When you're with your children, even very young ones, and you need to answer a business call or text, excuse yourself and go to a different room. By doing so, you're modeling intentional, voluntary attention, and also letting them know that you respect the "air space" that you share. (You'll be particularly happy to have this practice in place when your kids are teens and you're not as enthused about their music as they are.)

When I've discussed these practices with parents, occasionally they object, making the valid point that their children need to learn that an adult has to be responsible about his job. It's what puts food on the table, and these are opportunities for kids to get that message.

I agree. It's a valid point. It's also true, though, that at this stage in their brain development, that message is too removed and abstract to register as strongly as the more immediate, concrete one they're receiving: "Mom and Dad do this. I will, too."

Something else successful parents say is, "I'm teaching her multitasking when I do that." Children don't understand that multitasking has a time and a place. Plus, children need to build reasonably strong voluntary attention *before* they attempt to divide it. When you multitask in your child's presence, she's sees what it looks like from the outside, not the inner tasks of rapid, accurate prioritization that are required of a skillful multitasker.

Pablo Picasso once said, "Learn the rules like a pro, so you can break them like an artist." The rules of attention work the same way. It's only after your child builds voluntary attention that she can effectively judge when and how to multitask without overlooking important details and considerations.

When we multitask, we feel like we're getting more done. The ability to work from home is a job requirement for many, especially anyone with career ambition. Entrepreneurs will defend the practice, claiming it's how they built their businesses. But the question remains: what do our children perceive and how does that impact the development of their voluntary attention?

CONSIDER THAT THE BRAIN IS BUILT FOR MIMICRY

Scientists have studied what common sense tells us: children learn by watching. They've even identified how the brain makes this happen.

Research on imitative behavior began in 1961, when psychologist Albert Bandura observed preschoolers individually through a one-way mirror.[2] First, a child was left to play with toys in one corner of a room. In another corner, an adult, also surrounded by toys, was either aggressive or indifferent to a Bobo doll. (A Bobo doll is an inflatable clownlike figure, weighted at the bottom, so when it's punched, it rights itself back up.) Then, the child was taken to another room with toys, and this time the child's toys included a Bobo doll. If the adult had been aggressive in the other room, now that it was his turn, the child was aggressive, too. If the adult had acted indifferently, so did the child.

Behavioral scientists called this "social learning," and forty years later, with more advanced knowledge and technology, neuroscientists identified the biological mechanism responsible for it—namely, mirror neurons.[3]

A mirror neuron fires both when you perform an action and when you observe the same action performed. Mirror neurons help explain why you feel excited when your favorite team gets on the scoreboard. You, yourself, didn't score a point, but a team you identify with did, and you feel the excitement. When we imitate each other's body language, mirror neurons are at work.

Mirror neurons explain why it's easier for your child to concentrate on his homework if you're in the same room concentrating on your work, too, and also why it matters that you don't text or answer your phone during this time. If you let your devices command your attention, your child's mirror neurons will register your action. Your decisions will strengthen your child's digital habits, for better or for worse.

Also be aware of how mirror neurons affect your behavior. Scientists call this reciprocal effect "resonant activity." If other family members in your home are at their screens, notice how you may feel the urge for a screen, too.

PAY UNDIVIDED ATTENTION TO YOUR CHILD

A little boy I saw in my practice had to hold back his tears as he told his mother that he wished she hadn't gone to his Little League game. She was devastated but she understood. He'd fielded a hard-to-reach ball and turned a would-be scoring hit for the opposing team into a critical out. Not being a particularly athletic boy, he was ecstatic. When the play was complete, he looked up to see his mother looking down at her smartphone.

She apologized to him, explaining that returning the e-mail was important to her job—but then confided to me that she felt awful because, in fact, the e-mail had been unnecessary. She'd been catching up on her e-mails at games, always stopping when her son was up at bat. But when her son's team was in the field, she didn't always stop to look up when she heard cheering. Her son, far in the outfield, was seldom part of the action. She said lots of parents did this and she didn't think it was such a big deal. But then her son said every time he thought about the play now, he thought about her missing it. He wished she wasn't part of his memory of that otherwise glorious moment. He was being honest, not manipulative, and she knew it. He felt sad and angry, and she understood why. Missing the play stood for the bigger picture of the decisions she'd been making.

The venerable Buddhist master Thich Nhat Hanh tells us that "the most precious gift we can offer anyone is our attention." Intuitively, children know this, especially young children. Notice how when you answer the phone, a young child, sensing the potential unavailability of something of great value, will immediately manufacture a need for you to pay attention to him.

It's not practical, nor is it desirable, to give our children all of our undivided attention all of the time that we're with them. Until their brain grows enough for them to fully develop empathy, they're naturally egocentric and don't need further proof that the universe revolves around them. But when we're with our children, our decisions about reacting to digital devices warrant our consideration of effects on them that last much longer than an unanswered cellphone.

Often, we don't realize that as parents, we have real power to unintentionally hurt our children's feelings—for example, by answering a text when we're face-to-face with them. Unlike adults, who can take action when they feel slighted, a child doesn't understand why he feels badly. What he does know is how to imitate and, given time, he'll do what you do right back to you, also unintentionally, as a self-protection.

PRACTICE VOLUNTARY ATTENTION WHEN YOUR CHILD IS AROUND

Sometimes we're not face-to-face with our children, but we're still in close enough proximity that we serve as models for them. When we're in another room, they know if we're reading a book or we're watching TV. In fact, background TV, often presumed to be benign, may be a stealth attention snatcher to everyone in the house.

On my intake form, one of the questions I ask parents is how much TV their child watches. One parent, whose child had attention problems, reported none. One week, I had to call her regarding a schedule change, and in the background, I heard the TV. The next time we spoke, I asked her about it. She told me it was just the little eight-inch TV in her kitchen. She keeps it on mostly for news.

I realized I'd been neglecting the impact of background TV and probably so had many of the parents I counsel. When I looked into it, I learned that negative effects of background TV are well demonstrated. Studies specifically link background TV with lowered sustained attention[4] and reduced performance on tests of mental abilities[5] in children. The prevalence of background TV is high—an average of nearly four hours per day in homes with children eight months to eight years of age. A 2012 review article in *Pediatrics* examined studies of background TV and concluded by urging pediatricians to make an effort to reduce children's exposure to it by instructing parents to routinely turn it off.[6]

In addition to background TV noise, attention is also weakened by the presence of a smartphone—for example, at the table. Although no one is actively using it, this "background tech" causes everyone to have, in the back of their minds, the anticipation that it can go off at any moment. If it's your phone, a part of your attention is tethered to it and your children notice this. Observe the difference when no smartphone is in view. In Step Six (chapter 9), we'll talk more about tech-free family dinners.

PRACTICE VOLUNTARY ATTENTION WHEN YOUR CHILD IS NOT AROUND

Does it matter if *you* don't have voluntary attention as a goal for yourself as long as your child doesn't know?

Your child knows. Children have antennae for hypocrisy. Psychologist Catherine Steiner-Adair specializes in the impact of technology on families. She says that as soon as children know the meaning of the word "hypocrite," they use it to describe their parents when it comes to screentime. She describes children's feelings about vying with digital devices for their parents' attention as the "new sibling rivalry."[7]

Jim Henson, the brilliant creator of the Muppets, had a deep and intuitive understanding of children. He said, "The attitude you have as a parent is what your kids will learn from more than what you tell them. They don't remember what you try to teach them. They remember who you are."

To improve your own habits with digital media, make a commitment to practice the first exercise in Step One, "See through the Lens of Voluntary or Involuntary Attention," *for yourself* (as well as your child) as a rule. You'll find yourself giving greater thought to your decisions to use attention snatchers. A pleasant bonus is that when you use one intentionally, you'll feel freer to enjoy the experience.

In the next chapter you'll learn about the 3 Rs of good attention: running, reflection, and rethinking screentime. When you read about ways to put these 3 Rs into practice, be thinking about yourself as well as your child.

6

Step Three
Practice the 3 Rs of Good Attention

Actions speak louder than words,
but not nearly so often.
—Mark Twain

When you ask yourself the "What am I *not* doing now?" question, chances are the answer is one of the 3 Rs of good attention.

The 3 Rs of Good Attention

***R**unning, or any kind of physical exercise, especially outdoors*
***R**eflection, which includes quiet time, thoughtful conversation, and deep reading*
***R**ethinking Screentime, awareness of its impact on voluntary attention and the choice to use it intentionally*

Helping your child learn to practice each of the 3 Rs is good parenting for reasons that have nothing to do with attention. Promoting physical exercise fights childhood obesity; encouraging quiet time and reading increases children's understanding of themselves and their world; and supervision of screentime reduces children's risk for exposure to inappropriate content, predators, cyberbullying, and the like. But powerful evidence also shows that each of these practices—which are declining due to children's increasing use of technology—significantly benefits the development of voluntary attention.

Although the 3 Rs sound simple enough, they're easier said than done in today's busy, noisy world. They get lost in the decisions parents have to make every day. Do you keep your child sitting at a desk to finish schoolwork or send him outside to get some exercise and fresh air? When your child reads posts and writes texts, isn't that better than no reading or writing at all? If your child is good at video games, he has the chance to excel at skills like spatial learning, which are important in fields like science and technology. Don't you want him to play as much as possible so he can compete with other future engineers and programmers who play these games at advanced levels, too?

Each of the 3 Rs builds voluntary attention skills and helps your child develop the brain pathways that support them. *Consistency is the key.* When you and your children practice the 3 Rs consistently, they'll soon bring benefits into your home and will serve your children well into adulthood.

1. RUNNING

> As one parent told me, she now lives by the rule, "Tire them out before they tire you out." At homework time, her son used to wear her down with questions, complaints, excuses, distractions, and other sundry delay tactics. Now she scoots him out the door before he sits down to work. "He still dawdles, but not nearly as much—and with a whole lot less attitude."

One of the first things I learned about working with kids who have attention problems is that they're usually better listeners if they've had time to play outside. This can be a tough sell to parents who, understandably, are afraid their children will get too wound up and never settle down (which is true if a child is overstimulated for other reasons—for instance, having consumed too much sugar).

Exercise scientists have shown that physical activity helps children pay attention immediately afterward. For example, in a 2013 study reported to the American College of Sports Medicine, fourth and fifth grade students who exercised vigorously for ten minutes before a math exam scored significantly higher than a comparable group of fourth and fifth graders who were sedentary during that time.[1]

Much of the research supporting the cognitive benefits of physical exercise is summarized by psychiatrist John Ratey in *Spark*, his seminal book on the link between exercise and the brain.[2] In one study, students who took an aerobic phys ed class during first period were split into two groups. One group took a literacy class during second period and the other, during eighth period. Both groups showed improvement in reading and comprehension, but the second-period group, who had the class immediately following aerobic exercise, performed best.

This study was part of a larger educational experiment that teaches physical fitness to high school students in a school district on the outskirts of Chicago. The program resulted in dramatically higher standardized test scores for its participants. Ratey's book goes on to describe important new research that explains the biology behind these encouraging results. Scientists had assumed that the effects of exercise would show up in the motor cortex of the brain, but they were surprised to discover critical changes in the hippocampus, the part of the brain responsible for learning and memory. In addition, body movement generates an important brain chemical called "brain-derived neurotrophic factor" (BDNF),[3] which Ratey calls "Miracle-Gro for the brain."

A 2013 study in the *Journal of Pediatrics* showed that for fourth through eighth graders, aerobic fitness predicted higher standardized scores in math and reading.[4] These results were consistent with the findings of a review article that analyzed and summarized the research that has been published to date on this topic. The article concluded that aerobic exercise improves executive functions, including voluntary attention, in children, adolescents, and adults.[5]

Ironically, the very thing that can improve our brain's decision-making about our use of technology—physical exercise—is crowded out of our lives by our use of technology. Here are some suggestions for getting it back in.

Find the Right Activities

> We felt it was important for him to play a team sport to learn good sportsmanship and be part of a group effort. We tried lacrosse, soccer, and baseball, but he got too distracted by the other players, which caused him to make mistakes. His teammates wanted to like him but they also wanted to win. You could tell they wished he wasn't there. He wished he wasn't there, too.
>
> Each time, we made him stick it out for the full season. By the end, he was miserable and we were exhausted. He's a runner now and it's great. Next year, he'll start middle school and join a cross-country team. He's more suited to that kind of team experience.

It's good to have a vision of what you hope your child might like, and it's natural to feel elated when your child plays the same sport you played. But having a preconceived notion of what your child *should* like is asking to learn a lesson in how life works, the hard way. Your child has her own athletic aptitudes and interests, which can range from ballet to break-dancing, extreme sports to yoga, or Xbox Kinect to Wii workouts.

Your child's favorite sport may vary according to her growing abilities, what's trending with her age group, what her closest friends play, or the phase of the moon. You've got to make judgment calls when she wants to start or stop a sport. Whatever you decide, help your child feel good about the decision.

Encourage your child to try new activities. Each one provides new information and gets you closer to finding out what your child genuinely likes. Make it easy to start and enjoyable to stick with it. No matter the sport, game, or exercise, there's an app for it. Just make sure your child is committed, dressed, and ready to go before reaching for a digital device. That way, she won't wind up playing video games instead of tracking her run.

Keep gear like jump ropes, balls, and bicycles easily accessible. Give them their best shot at competing with electronic media that's just a click away.

- Don't buy into a low-energy "Do we have to?" resistance.
- Do keep a high energy "Let's do it!" forward movement.

Be Careful about Competition

Some kids thrive on competition, some shy away from it, and just about every kid—actually every one of us—needs to keep it in perspective. Competition makes organized sports more exciting. It can be a healthy way for kids to learn how to lose, how to win, and how to play fairly. But ask any coach or referee if sometimes parents can get too worked up about the outcome of a game or a play on the field.

Competition can be a motivator, but encourage your child to go for her personal best. If your child ran a half-mile last month, a better goal for her this month is to run it faster or go farther, not to beat someone else's time or distance.

Some parents feel that this attitude is for wimps or that it's OK for recreational sports but not for serious athletes. As it happens, elite athletes who compete at the highest levels use this strategy. They know that it's a costly distraction to waste any of their attention on someone else's game. Every smidgen of their focus is on achieving their own best performance.[6]

Using only competition to motivate kids has the potential to backfire, especially for young children and beginners. You may get an immediate surge of interest, but it's not sustainable. Over time it takes the fun out of the game. It robs kids of the joy of moving their bodies, embarasses them if they make mistakes, and causes them to measure their worth in comparison to others, instead of being their best selves. This is particularly true with siblings who have different talents and gifts.

Kids are forced to compete in school for grades, test scores, and college admissions. They'll keep up an active lifestyle if it helps them to release their pressure, not add to it.

- Don't put too much emphasis on a final score.
- Do emphasize your child's effort, attitude, and willingness to practice.

Participate

When your children are young, invite them with you for a short run or a swim or whatever you do for exercise. They may not pursue your sport in the future, but their earliest memories of physical exercise will be happy ones with you.

As your children start to follow their own interests, be active with them. Play catch or one-on-one basketball, but let them take the lead.

Be sensitive to when it's time to back away and let them shine without you. Hopefully, you'll share a lifelong interest in staying active together, but give them their space. Participate in new ways. Be a good listener, enjoy their stories, and keep a place in your home for pictures of them in their team uniform or doing a kickflip at the skate park.

- Don't tell your older children how to improve in their favorite sport.
- Do find resources for them—classes, teams, rec centers, camps, trails, parks.

Let Your Child Decide (Sort Of)

Kyle, a high school sophomore, and his worried parents were referred to me when he was suspended for skipping school. Kyle had once been a good student. Now he squeaked by with decent grades, mostly due to missed and incomplete assignments and being late or absent from class. He spent most of his after-school time on Second Life, an online virtual world in which a user creates an avatar (a Second Life character), builds whatever he wants, meets other avatars whose users are currently online, and explores as he wishes.

At first, Kyle's parents thought Second Life was a good thing for Kyle because it seemed to keep him safe and make him happy. His friends from middle school were now hanging out at the mall and had gotten into trouble for shoplifting. Kyle's parents were glad he wasn't with them. But as Kyle began to spend more time in his virtual world, they could feel him gradually pull away from them and also from his remaining interest in school.

Kyle's mom started to work from home as much as possible so she could keep an eye on her son. Also, she wanted to get him out of the house, which was easier said than done. Second Life was about the only thing Kyle looked forward to anymore. He was a skinny, likeable kid, but somewhat guarded and nervous. As I got to know Kyle better, I realized there was a reason he'd skipped school that he wouldn't talk about, and I could see that on Second Life—and not at school—he felt emotionally safe and connected to others.

A few weeks after his suspension, a student anonymously reported that Kyle had been cornered by a bully and threatened at knifepoint. Kyle wasn't hurt physically, but the invisible wall he'd been building around him was now becoming impenetrable. I asked Kyle what he needed to feel safe again, and he told me that the world was not safe, so why pretend.

Kyle's dad offered him a gym membership and some personal training sessions. Kyle declined but still took his dad's lead. He walked into a martial arts studio one day and quietly watched a class. He enrolled, which proved to be a watershed event in his young life. He practiced daily, tested for belts, and became proficient. Gradually, he also started to improve his grades and talk about college. Eventually, his reliance on Second Life faded away.

A dramatic change like Kyle's is unusual, but when a kid commits to physical activity, a noticeable change for the better usually takes place.

So how do you get a kid to commit? What if your child is stuck in her sedentary ways? How can you get her up and moving?

As with Kyle, the more choice a child has in a decision, the more likely she is to stick with it. One strategy is to offer a "structured choice." In other words, give your child two or more choices, any of which are acceptable to you. For example, "This season do you want to sign up for swimming or soccer or softball?" Or, "Hey, the dog could use a nice, long walk to the park this afternoon. Do you want to take him now or later, as a break from your homework?"

Expect resistance at first—"Come on, Mom. I've got stuff to do." Don't take the bait and start arguing or explaining. Stay steadfast and kind. You're on the same side, doing what's best for your child. In a caring voice, ask her, "By what time, honey?" Your goal is to get her to make a specific commitment but still give her some face-saving choice in the matter.

- Don't get caught in your child's resistance.
- Do be pleasantly persuasive and give your child structured choice.

Stay Strong

Remember, all you need to do is help your child get started. Physical activity produces endorphins and enkephalins, the natural opiates of the body. Once your child is active, biology takes over and she'll be riding her own natural high. Physical activity becomes its own reward. Numerous studies have shown that regular aerobic exercise relieves depression and anxiety and increases resilience to stress. For example, for adults (average weight 150 pounds), walking fast for thirty-five minutes per day five times a week, or sixty minutes per day three times a week, significantly decreased symptoms of moderate clinical depression.[7]

If you lack conviction, your child will sense this and test you until you give in. Do what you need to do to fortify your own resolve. Stay focused on the benefits of exercise. Join with other parents who are also committed to fitness goals for their families. Notice the positive effects of exercise on your own health, stamina, and ability to sustain your attention, and keep that forefront in your mind. Your child's belief that exercise is worth the effort begins with your belief and actions that tell her that it's so.

Based on research findings, the World Health Organization recommends a minimum of sixty minutes per day of moderate to vigorous physical exercise for children ages five to seventeen years.[8]

- Don't be dissuaded by your child's initial resistance.
- Do remind yourself: "It will turn out well . . . as soon as we're past the getting-started part."

Buy a Pedometer

If you and your family are sedentary, one of the easiest ways to get started is to buy a simple, inexpensive pedometer. More expensive motion-detecting wristbands and computerized wristwatches are available and come with helpful software that graphs your child's progress. But to get things under way, a twenty-dollar pedometer fits the bill.

Use it yourself, first. Put it on in the morning and record your total number of steps each night. It won't be long before you know how many steps you average per day. Then set a modest goal for just a few hundred steps more. Don't judge or criticize or be concerned about exact accuracy; just write down that number every night. Notice how just by wearing it, you become more aware of staying active.

Once you've established the habit for yourself, get a pedometer for your child, too. Use your own experience to guide you to make it a game. Modify its use to after school and weekends (so your child doesn't have to wear it at school unless she wants to). Be creative about ways to rack up high numbers. Walk to the store together. Discover a new trail. Mall walk in inclement weather. Celebrate a ten-thousand-step day! Make it fun—no guilt trips for messing up. Every day's a new day, a fresh start.

- Don't expect too much too soon.
- Do be realistic and take the first step today.

Play Outside and Enjoy Nature

One afternoon last year, a power outage in our neighborhood lasted for hours. All through the afternoon and evening, we heard the joyful sounds of children's laughter outside. The next day it was gone. Children don't play much outside any more. "I'd rather play inside," Richard Louv quotes a little boy in *Last Child in the Woods,* "where the electrical outlets are."[9]

Louv observes, "There's no denying the benefits of the Internet. But electronic immersion, without a force to balance it, creates a hole in the boat—draining our ability to pay attention, to think clearly, to be productive and creative."[10] Louv makes a strong argument that the power of nature is the best force to restore this balance.

In a nationwide study of five- to eighteen-year-old children diagnosed with attention problems, exposure to ordinary natural settings in after-school and weekend activities resulted in a significant reduction of symptoms.[11] Other studies have shown similar effects—for example, improvements in attention span after walks in a park.[12] We'll discuss more about the impact of nature on attention in Step Six (chapter 9).

Louv points out that parents are worried about the safety of children in playgrounds and parks today. Instead of being a reason to abandon the great outdoors, that could be a reason to accompany children and enjoy being outside together. Make it a rule not to pass up a chance to be outdoors with your child.

In an ad for a pickup truck on TV right now, you see a dad and his reluctant son heading out for a camping trip. As you start to watch, you know this story has a happy ending and it's not just because that's what sells more trucks. The dad exudes a quiet confidence. He's certain that nature will win his son over as it did for him when he was a boy. As they set out, he's grinning for both of them. It's in his knowing smile that you sense a happy ending is on its way.

Find your knowing smile and get out into nature with your child. In the words of Albert Einstein, "Look deep into nature and then you will understand everything better."

- Don't stay indoors when you and your child can be outside.
- Do share the beauty and wonder of nature with your child every chance you get.

2. REFLECTION

> I've taught college for almost thirty years. There always have been some students who think more deeply than others. You'd see it in class discussions and when you read their papers. But now, so many students give answers that lack depth. What's new and concerns me most, though, is that they don't know it. Even when you try to explain it to them, they don't see that they're not focusing deeply.

I was conducting a webinar for educators last fall when a professor shared this observation. It was followed by overwhelming agreement from the other participants. What these professors had to say jibes with statistics. For example, abstract vocabulary scores on college admission tests have hit a record-breaking low.[13] One explanation is that more students are going to college so the norms are adjusting themselves down. But another is the fast pace and digital habits that characterize the formative years leading up to college. There's little chance for students to learn how to slow down and reflect. Our "always-on" culture conditions them to feel restless unless they're highly stimulated. It sends them a nonstop message that quiet time has no value when, in fact, the opposite is true. A child's growing brain needs quiet time to develop executive functions, especially voluntary attention.

As a guest on a late-night talk show, comedian Louis C.K. explained why he won't get smartphones for his kids.[14] When you feel the least bit alone, he says, instead of letting yourself have that experience, you send a text to fifty people. Someone texts you back and you feel better right away. Then someone cooler texts you back and you forget about the first guy. This reminded me of something that comedian Sid Caesar once said: "Comedy has to be based on truth. You take the truth and you put a little curlicue at the end." The curlicued truth of the matter is that kids growing up with technology today get the benefit of instant relief from loneliness but at the cost of knowing how to be alone. They miss the depth of thought and feeling that solitude can bring.

In *Seven Habits of Highly Effective People*, business guru Stephen Covey makes a useful distinction between managers and leaders.[15] Managers, Covey says, find the best ways to accomplish things; leaders decide what needs to be accomplished. He talks about managers cutting through a jungle with a machete, while leaders climb trees to determine if it's the right jungle.

Our children need to become both managers and leaders of their lives, but managing is taking over. Their lives are consumed with managing texts and e-mails, photos and playlists, files and apps, and their online persona. They seldom sit quietly long enough to appreciate a top-of-the-tree perspective so they can intentionally *lead* their lives. Attention snatchers are stealing their quiet time, and our quiet time, too. Without it, how can any of us lead, as well as manage, our busy lives?

Typically, the young adults I see in my practice are driven by to-do lists and FOMO (fear of missing out), which we'll discuss in chapter 11. It's a struggle for them to settle down long enough to reflect on what direction they want their lives to go. The anxiety they feel when they're quiet is palpable. They're springloaded to release their inner tension by texting, gaming, or going online.

We need quiet time, so that within ourselves, the voice of management doesn't drown out the voice of leadership. Covey relates what happens when a treetop leader calls out, "Wrong jungle." "Shut up," the efficient managers call back, "We're making progress!"

Value Quiet Time

At school, children are rewarded for acing timed tests that measure how quickly, not how deeply, they can think. In the classroom, if they take too long to answer a question or participate in a discussion, they may be labeled as "slow processers." In her best-selling book *Quiet*, Susan Cain calls our value system "the extrovert ideal."[16] In other words, action trumps contemplation. She cites studies in which talkative people are rated as smarter and more likeable and introverts are seen as bland. And yet, as Cain reminds us, "Some of our greatest ideas, art, and inventions—from the theory of evolution to van Gogh's sunflowers to the personal computer—came from quiet and cerebral people who knew how to tune in to their inner worlds and the treasures to be found there."

Are you too nervous to sit still? Quite possibly you're locked into the mind-set that time is scarce. Psychologists who specialize in this area have shown how the perception of scarcity impairs judgment.[17] In life, there will always be more things to do than time to do them. So what matters is good judgment about your priorities. And for that, you need time to be quiet and think deeply.

- Don't fall into the trap of perceiving time as scarce.
- Do learn to respect the power of silence and stillness.

Don't Give Quiet Time a Bad Rap

What are the hidden messages we send to our children in our everyday responses to their behaviors? For example, what do you say when your child says, "I'm bored"?

Children have probably been saying "I'm bored" since the days when they waited while their cave parents rubbed two sticks together to make fire. What's different today is that "I'm bored" is often code for "I want to watch TV" or "play video games" or "go on my iPad." Ordinary life seems dull. Think of what it feels like when you exit off a highway. You may be driving at thirty miles per hour, but it feels like you're hardly moving because moments ago you were driving about twice as fast. Your kids feel this way when they're not at a screen and need to come down from a steady stream of "high-stim" (that is, highly stimulating) activity.

Have rules in place about your child's use of digital media—more about that later in this chapter—and don't break them because your child tells you he's bored. If you do, you're training him to become bored so that he can watch TV.

Refrain from feeling responsible and jumping into action at the words "I'm bored." Shake the feeling that it's up to you to keep your child busy every waking moment. It's OK for him to flounder a bit. You can give him some guidance but remain clear that it's his task, not yours, to discover the hidden treasures of his downtime. If he senses that you're taking the bait, offering suggestion after suggestion, he'll outlast you in a game of "Yes, but . . ." and before long, he'll be watching TV.

Try some creative responses that act as catalysts for children to come up with their own ideas. Tell a preschooler, "I'm happy you're using your words," then redirect him to a choice of age-appropriate quiet-time activities. Tell a school-age child you remember being bored as a kid, too. "It's a great feeling to have nothing that you have to do!" Ask a teen, "I wonder what Elon Musk [or his favorite musician or comic book artist] does when he has that feeling?" Of course, even if it sparks a new idea for him, it's compulsory that he rolls his eyes and answers, "I don't know," giving you the chance to practice your most serene Buddha smile.

Another prime example of unintentionally training a child to dislike being alone is when the practice of "time out" is used as a punishment in anger, instead of a teaching tool for your child to learn to calm down and reflect on his transgression. For instance, if your child is blatantly disobedient—defies you by turning the TV on when he's not supposed to—you're likely to feel provoked and tempted to yell, "Turn that TV off or you're headed for a time out that you won't forget."

Compare that to walking into the room, turning the TV off, making eye contact with your child, and calmly saying, "What you're doing is very wrong" and following up with corrective action.

- *For a preschooler*, say, "We both feel happier when you're a better listener. It's time to go to your room, so you can remember what it feels like to do the right thing." If necessary, take his hand and quietly walk him there. After a few minutes, join your child and give him the chance to apologize and promise not to do it again, if he hasn't done so already.
- *For a school-age child,* suggest that he use the time to think things over and write a note of apology, with a promise not to do it again.
- *For an older child*, have him write out the reasons for the rule and a plan for how he can keep it in the future—for example, by having a list of other things to do when he's tempted to turn on the TV.

Older children need to have a say in the making of rules about digital media to begin with. Otherwise, their apologies and plans to do better in the future won't be genuine. (We'll take a closer look at kids having a say in making rules later in this chapter.)

It can be tough to stay calm when your child defies you, but keep in mind that quiet works better than loud for effecting change that endures. Using time out in anger as a punishment will change your child's *performance* but not his *learning*. He'll continue the transgression, being more careful not to get caught. The neural activity for changing a performance out of fear is in the reactive part of his brain, not the part that's responsible for learning.

On the other hand, time out as a learning tool can make a lasting change. When your child has to think of what he needs to do differently, he activates the learning part of his brain that's connected to logic and reason. He uses the time to come up with a plan for how to resist the marshmallow of the moment. His plan may or may not work next time, but he's taking responsibility, thinking it over, realizing he has choices, and putting thought and effort into how to make the best one.

- Don't unintentionally give quiet time a bad name by using it punitively.
- Do teach your child accountability by having him reflect on his actions quietly.

Learn about Mindfulness

Recent years have seen a surge of interest in a practice called "mindfulness," the act of silently directing your attention to the present moment with unconditional acceptance for what is. In mindfulness meditation, you continually catch your mind when it starts to wander and bring your awareness back to the present—which you can do, for example, by focusing on your breathing.

Most people find that the hardest part is letting go of judgments—good or bad. "I'm pretty cool, learning to meditate" or "This is a stupid exercise." Either way, you're still sitting in judgment of yourself instead of staying focused on present-moment sensations such as breathing. The key is to allow your "narrative" to pass.

To an outside observer, someone practicing meditative mindfulness appears to be in a passive state, but mindfulness is actually a rigorous form of voluntary attention. Your effort to bring your awareness back to the present moment, and away from distracting thoughts and feelings, is ongoing. In the same way that weight-resistance training at a gym strengthens muscles, your voluntary attention carries the load, resisting distraction and growing stronger each time you practice.

Mindfulness meditation is rooted in the Buddhist tradition, but training in its modern form is now offered at universities, businesses, government agencies, hospitals, prisons, and more. One reason for its current popularity is the media coverage that's been given to research findings that document its benefits. In addition to stress management, recovery from injury, reduction of pain, and other health benefits such as smoking cessation, mindfulness meditation has been shown to improve overall control of attention and to strengthen the neural pathways that support it.[18]

In my practice, I've found that some kids who've attended classes in mindfulness meditation take to it and others do not. Children are more likely to practice mindfulness if their parents practice it, too. Many apply the principles in ways that suit them—for example, adapting their practice to walking meditations, or making a habit of nonjudgmental acceptance, a term that deserves further clarification.

Nonjudgmental acceptance does not mean that you stop exercising good judgment. Paradoxically, nonjudgmental acceptance helps you make better judgments. *When you let go of expectations of the way things should be, you're in a better place to deal with them the way that they are.* For example, if your child refuses to stop playing a video game when it's time for him to do so, you're likely to be clearer about the best course of action to correct his mistake if you let go of the loaded expectation that he shouldn't make mistakes like that.

The practice of mindfulness strengthens voluntary attention and improves other executive functions including decision-making. It develops several key parts of the brain including the prefrontal cortex.[19]

Many resources are available to learn more about the practice of mindfulness. A good place to start is by watching, listening, or reading materials about mindfulness-based stress reduction (MBSR), a program founded by physician Jon Kabat-Zinn, a professor at the University of Massachusetts Medical School.[20] Thich Nhat Hanh, a Buddhist monk, and Kabat-Zinn have been instrumental in combining Eastern practices of meditation with Western medicine and collaborating with scientists who are documenting rather remarkable results.[21]

If you related to being locked into the perception that time is scarce (discussed earlier in this chapter), mindfulness techniques have your name on them. In the Notes section, you'll find the link to one of my favorite introductory videos—Kabat-Zinn giving a talk at Google headquarters in Palo Alto, California.[22]

Research on teaching mindfulness to children is showing promising results.[23] An increasing number of young people are drawn to yoga, which is a related practice, and in youthful Silicon Valley, mindfulness training is thriving.[24] In the words of Thich Nhat Hanh, "We have more possibilities available in each moment than we realize."

- Don't dismiss mindfulness as a fad. It's now evidence-based.
- Do learn more about mindfulness to see if it could be right for your child and you.

Teach and Practice Active Listening

Texting, tweeting, posting, chatting, and other forms of online communication train kids to keep messages short, ignore much of what others say, and pay more attention to transmitting than receiving communications. Consequently, in face-to-face interactions, kids tune out cues, including signals that they need to be better listeners.

Actively listening to others requires patience, develops empathy, builds voluntary attention, and starts with a child's ability to quiet himself. Gently remind young children to use their inside voice and their listening ears. If your preschooler needs frequent reminders, prevent nagging by creating a hand signal—maybe a quick tug on your ear—sent with a gentle smile.

Be sure you're modeling good listening skills yourself, especially when you're distracted by a digital device. If your child is in the habit of not listening, don't yell at him when he ignores you. Instead, ask him, in a kind voice, to repeat what you just said. This technique can be highly effective but only with the right intonation. It's not "What did I just say?"with a wrinkled brow in an irritated voice. It's "Honey, tell me what I just said," with a smile and a loving, I'm-rooting-for-you-to-get-this voice. If he can't tell you because he wasn't listening, make eye contact with him and ask him again. If he's getting embarrassed, give it a rest. Try saying good-naturedly, "That's why we have two ears and only one mouth."

For very young kids who need to learn how to listen, consider making a game of using a "talking stick." Let them know that it's a time-honored tradition handed down from many Native American tribes.

The person who has the stick talks while everyone else listens. You can adapt the rules to fit your needs—for instance, use a time limit for each talker if necessary. Any handy stick will do—a pencil, a spoon, whatever's in reach. If you've used a talking stick at least once in a relaxed setting—for example, making up a silly story together—it will be easier to use it when tempers flare—for example, when siblings fight.

To get older kids to switch from "transmit" to "receive," try structuring the conversation with this simple rule. Before you speak, reflect back to the other person, in your own words, what you heard him say. It may seem awkward at first, but soon, everyone catches on and likes feeling listened to.

You can introduce active listening in whatever way works for you. Since I use it with the families I see in counseling, it's easy for them to do it at home, too. One mom I know told me that her company had sponsored a communications seminar that taught a similar method. When she returned, she taught it to her family and they use it now when they discuss potentially volatile topics like house rules and money.

Active listening is a useful practice if a conversation in your home begins to generate more heat than light, but only if your child's emotional brain hasn't already taken over. If it has, you'll need to wait until his thinking brain is more accessible.

Sometimes when I introduce active listening, families will say that it doesn't sound like a real conversation or that it feels strange or uncomfortable. Active listening requires more patience than we're used to. Those feelings are a sign that you're trying something new. Feeling discomfort means you're outside of your comfort zone where real change takes place.

Let's say you and your preteen daughter are arguing about how much TV she's been watching and the quarrel is escalating. Here's an example of what it might sound like:

Child: "That's not fair, Mom. If I do all my homework, I should be able to watch as much TV as I want."

Parent: "Hey, instead of arguing, let's do something different. Let's take turns talking and listening. When you talk, I'll listen to you, and the way you'll know I listened is that I'll tell you what I heard you say. Then it'll be my turn to talk, and when I do, you'll listen, and tell me what you heard me say, before you talk again."

Child: "That's stupid, Mom."

Parent: "Let's try it anyway. And let's keep what we're saying kind of short, so the other person can remember it. But it doesn't have to be word-for-word. It'll be in our own words. OK?"

Child: "It's too weird."

Parent: "Seriously, I want us to try this."

Child: "Whatever."

Parent: "Do you want to go first, or do you want me to go first?"

Child: "This is your thing. You go first."

Parent: "OK. I'm really glad you're willing to try this."

Child: "So what am I supposed to say?"

Parent: "What you just heard me say."

Child: "What? Seriously? That you're glad we're doing whatever this is?"

Parent: "Yeah. And now you talk and I listen."

Child: "You treat me like a baby, Mom. I can't stand it."

Parent: "I heard you say that I treat you like a baby and you can't stand it."

Child: "Yeah."

Parent: "That's not my intention."

Child: "It doesn't matter whether you mean it or not."

Parent: "Honey, what did you hear me say?"

Child (rolling her eyes): "You don't mean to treat me like a baby."

Parent: "Yeah."

Child: "But you do. No one else has these stupid rules."

Parent: "You still feel I treat you like a baby and you're the only one your age with rules about TV."

Child: "That's right. And it's not fair!"

Parent: "Honey, I just told you what I heard you say. Now it's my turn to talk and your turn to listen. Ready? I don't see you as a baby. Remember, I let you go to the mall with your friends?"

Child (sighing): "You said you don't see me as a baby and you let me go to the mall with my friends." Mom nods. Child is quiet for a moment, then says, "OK. But that doesn't have anything to do with TV. Why are you being so mean?"

Parent: "You remembered that I let you go to the mall, but that has nothing to do with TV, and you wonder why I'm acting mean about this." Pauses and looks at her daughter who nods. "From where I sit, I'm not acting mean. I love you too much to see your beautiful brain turn into mush."

Child: "You are so acting mean. My brain is not turning into mush."

Parent: "What did you hear me say?"

Child: "That you don't think you're acting mean. You think you're doing it for my own good." Cracks a half-smile. "So maybe could you love me a few hours of TV less?"

Instead of ending in a shouting match, an argument that uses active listening, like this one, has a better chance of ending with parent and child amicably agreeing to disagree. In this case, the child accepts a good rule even if she does so reluctantly. Plus, she's exercising voluntary attention and working memory to improve her communication skills even in a state of anger. An exchange like this one strengthens important neural pathways for quiet, active listening.

Another pearl from the writings of Thich Nhat Hanh: "I am determined to practice deep listening. I am determined to practice loving speech." In a culture that values aggressively speaking up and speaking out, it takes determination to patiently listen and reflect on what the other person just said, instead of jumping to what it is we want to say next.

- Don't talk *at* each other.
- Do listen with your ears and your heart.

Understand Your Child's Reading Brain

Reading opens doors for our children, but only if they can comprehend and reflect on what they've read. Reading is entirely a learned process and your child's formative brain changes its own structure in response to his reading habits.

As cognitive scientist Maryanne Wolf points out, "We human beings were never born to read."[25] The human brain has a visual cortex, an auditory cortex, and a prefrontal cortex for executive functions like voluntary attention, but it has *no* "reading cortex." In Wolf's words, the reading brain is "a miracle that springs from the brain's unique capacity to rearrange itself to learn something new."

As your child reads more challenging material, his developing brain reorganizes critical areas in vision, language, and cognition. If your growing child concentrates and engages in "deep reading processes"—reflection, critical analysis, inference—his reading brain develops these networks. But, as Wolf observes, "There is no single reading brain template and the reading brain as we know it today never needs to develop."

When he's an adult, what will your child's reading brain look like? Will it be rich in deep-reading connections, allowing him to comprehend lengthy books of substance and draw wisdom from what he's read to apply to his own life? Or will his brain be limited to forming the connections he needs to scan while scrolling, tweeting, and texting as he watches TV?

Nicholas Carr, author of *The Shallows: What the Internet Is Doing to Our Brains,* acknowledges that power-browsing has been a godsend to him as a writer.[26] "Research that once required days in the stacks or periodical rooms of libraries can now be done in minutes," he observes. But he also discloses,

> I'm not thinking the way I used to think. I can feel it most strongly when I'm reading. Immersing myself in a book or a lengthy article used to be easy. . . . That's rarely the case anymore. Now my concentration often starts to drift after two or

> three pages. . . . The deep reading that used to come naturally has become a struggle.[27]

He goes on to report that his friends and associates—"literary types, most of them"—are having similar experiences. For example, Bruce Friedman, a pathologist, medical school faculty member, and blogger, said, "I can't read *War and Peace* anymore. I've lost the ability to do that." (By the way, does this seem like a long chapter to you? Me, too.)

Most likely, if Carr and Friedman made it their goal to start reading books of substance once again, they could recover their ability to read *War and Peace*. That's because when they were children as they read great literature, synapse by synapse, their brains built intricate connections and reorganized themselves, as Wolf described, to be able to comprehend a complex Russian novel. As adults, although these neural pathways may be weak or dormant from lack of use, they're established networks that can be reactivated with practice.

Children who grow up replacing deep reading with power-browsing will not establish these networks to begin with. Unlike Carr and Friedman, they can't regain an ability to read *War and Peace* if they didn't have it in the first place. If their brains rearrange themselves in childhood to support quick scanning but not deep reading, then, for all intents and purposes, reading *War and Peace* will not be a choice for them. It's up to us to encourage our children to read books of substance. It's a choice we make for them now that gives them greater choice in the future.

Scanning is a useful skill—indispensable in our world today. But unless your family lives under a rock, your child has already logged in hundreds of hours of scanning and will log in thousands more. Scanning requires a minimum of voluntary attention, so kids do it while they multitask. Our children are at no risk of failing to form brain connections that support it. The real question is, will they use scanning to complement reading or to replace it?

When it comes to the reading brain, the known evidence is clear.

If you encourage your child to read longer and more difficult material, and to comprehend and reflect on what he's read, you're taking less chance on how limited his reading brain will be when he's an adult.

- Don't take for granted that your child's reading brain will look like yours.
- Do be aware that your child's reading habits are shaping his brain in profound and lasting ways.

Don't Blur the Distinction between Scanning and Reading

According to a large national survey, 28 percent of youth ages nine to seventeen say that looking through posts on social networking sites such as Facebook counts as reading, and 15 percent of parents agree. One in four kids in this age bracket counts texting as reading, too.[28] But, as we discussed, inside your child's brain, scanning is *not* the same as deep reading.

In your house, do you use the term "scanning" when you refer to skimming through posts and texts and reserve the word "reading" for longer articles and books? Doing so may sound picky, but it promotes awareness.

This same survey shows that 86 percent of the kids report that they feel proud and have a sense of accomplishment when they finish reading a book. That's not the feeling you get from scanning, and when encouraging your child to read, you can capitalize on that.

To strengthen your children's motivation to read books, help them notice how good they feel about themselves when they're done reading. Emphasize your child's effort and perseverance, not how smart he is or how fast he can read.

- *That was a big book and you really stuck with it. I bet you feel great.*
- *You've got to feel so proud of yourself, finishing that book.*
- *You can feel really good about yourself. That's quite a book you just finished.*

It's best to emphasize your child's effort and not how smart he is, because you want to motivate him for the next book. Children who are praised because they're smart feel less motivated to try harder. They want to perform as well as they did when they earned your praise, but since being smart is beyond their control, they don't know what to do to keep it up. In fact, to them, if they look like they're trying too hard, you won't think they're so smart anymore.

However, when you let your child know that you've noticed his effort, he now has a very specific way to keep earning recognition—namely, he can keep trying hard. Stanford University psychologist Carol Dweck has spent decades documenting the ongoing success of "mastery" students, who believe that you need to do things to become smart, and the eventual downfall of "helpless" students, who believe you're either born smart or you aren't.[29] Children with a mastery mind-set want to take on tougher challenges. Children who believe that being smart is an entity prefer to repeat easier tasks that they know they can do.

It's best not to comment on how fast your child can read a book, as this encourages skimming and discourages reading for comprehension and pleasure.

- Don't confuse scanning and reading.
- Do help your child notice the personal satisfaction of reading a book.

Share the Joy of Reading with Your Child at Every Age

Interactive books now enable very young children to crack the code and learn to read on their own. "Read-aloud" features allow a child to hear a friendly, recorded voice reading to him while simultanously seeing each word light up, one by one, in sync with the recorded voice. A child can go back and repeat a passage as many times as he likes, or skip ahead, or start or stop whenever he wants. It's a brilliant application of technology that can help children become good readers at remarkably early ages.

When it comes to interactive books with read-aloud features, what are we *not* thinking of? While these books are extremely useful learning tools, they don't replace the warmth and security a child feels when a parent reads to him and the way that shapes a child's feelings about reading. Read-aloud features are best used in addition to parents reading to children, not in place of it. Based on research of early brain development, the American Academy of Pediatrics now recommends that parents start reading to their babies from birth.[30]

Does it matter if you read to your child from an ebook or a print book? Each type of book has its own merit. Ebooks are a huge convenience, easy to download and take on a trip. Dictionary features give children the ability to instantly discover the meanings of new words and concepts. Print books have a different type of physical presence and carry a different feeling, as children themselves have pointed out.

According to another, similar national survey, kids say they prefer ebooks when they're out and about and when they don't want their friends to know what they're reading, but that print is better for sharing with friends and reading at bedtime.[31] It strikes me as interesting that most children still prefer print books before going to sleep. While in the future this may change as parents read more ebooks to children at night, for now, print books are likely touchstones for children to feel tucked in and safe. Whether you use print or ebook media, reading together is a precious and short-lived opportunity to bond with your child and unite both of you with the pleasure of reading.

Any time, day or night, reading is a powerful builder of voluntary attention. Keep this in mind when you look at your child texting, playing games, or on social media, and ask yourself the question, "What is he *not* doing now?" If "reading a book" comes to mind, some follow-up questions are, "What book is he reading right now?" and "Where is it?"

Always have a book that your child loves nearby. Keep lots of good books where he can see them. Have a new book waiting when he finishes the one he's reading.

Express interest in his books. Most young children enjoy telling you about a book they're reading. Older kids may feel like you're butting in on something that's all their own or, even worse, interrogating them.

Timing, authenticity, your attitude, tone of voice, and word choice can make a big difference.

- *I read that book when I was your age. Mind if I page through it and see what comes back to me?*
- *Let's go online together and look at ebook downloads from the library tonight, so you'll have them for the trip tomorrow morning.*
- *That's an interesting title. What's it about?*

The survey also reported that the biggest influence on how much kids read is how much their parents read. Nothing else has as much impact, not even household income. With so much on our plates every day, we tend to feel guilty when we sit down and open a book. Yet it's a responsible thing for a parent to do.

If your child is having trouble settling down to do his homework and you want to sit in the same room with him (as we discussed in Step One, chapter 4), you can use the opportunity take out your book and read. Or just read when and where you can. Treat yourself to guilt-free reading because you're doing it for the sake of your child!

- Don't allow a day without a book in the house that your child wants to read.
- Do read books.

3. RETHINKING SCREENTIME

The third R stands for "rethinking screentime," so that we use it with awareness of both its pros and cons, particularly *its impact on your child's development of voluntary attention*. For example, while browsing websites that featured video game reviews for parents, I looked at the suggested ages for the popular puzzle-type game *Candy Crush Saga*. The range of ages and reasons for them varied. One site recommended age five and up, stating that the game taught flexibility and planning. Another recommended a minimum age of thirteen because it's "pushy" with its in-app purchases. The impact of the game on your child's voluntary attention was not considered as a factor at all. In fact, the quality score was high because the game captures a player's attention so well, a measure of how much involuntary, not voluntary, attention is involved. When considering screentime, it's up to you, as a parent, to take its impact on your child's voluntary attention into account, especially since no one else is.

When you're a parent, the third R extends to helping your child make responsible screentime choices, too. When she makes a poor choice, refrain from getting angry and instead look at her mistake as a *teachable moment.*

Help Your Child Become a Good Digital Citizen

Once, when visiting a model digital classroom, I spoke with a forward-thinking sixth-grade teacher who had an advanced degree in educational technology. She explained how the class used Google Docs to work on projects as a team. "What about back-channeling?" I asked. Other teachers had told me how difficult it is to use technology in the classroom if they can't turn off the various ways that kids can pass notes electronically during a lesson.

She smiled and replied, "My goal is to teach my students how to back-channel responsibly, not to forbid it." She went on to explain that she and many other teachers who specialize in ed tech have adopted this classroom policy. They monitor back-channeling and then discuss it with their students in class. They ask questions like, "Which comments were the most relevant and useful?" "Which ones were neither?" "Let's talk about that comment. It didn't contribute to the project directly, but it was funny—good for morale—and didn't take that long. Who thinks it was worth it?"

Her class also uses Edmodo, which is sometimes called "Facebook for schools." In a safe environment, closed to nonclass members, her students can discuss the relative merits of comments, photos, videos, and links that they've posted. They speak up when someone's post hurts someone else's feelings. When kids hear this feedback from other kids, they get it.

In the previously mentioned late-night talk show interview with Louis C.K. on why he won't get smartphones for his kids, the comedian also offers this reason for his decision. Children need to try things out with each other, he explains, so if a kid wants to try out his power over another kid, he says something mean, like "You're fat." But right away, he can see how the other kid's face scrunches up and he knows he's hurt him and feels bad for having done that. But if he texts it, he doesn't get that feedback. He feels powerful and will probably do it again.[32]

In this teacher's class, children have face-to-face conversations about their online comments, so they rethink commenting. This solves the problem that Louis C.K. so aptly described. It teaches kids how to text and comment with thought and sensitivity for others.

The teacher summed up this philosophy of education: "This is the world they live in, and it's our job to teach them how to live in it responsibly." She called it "becoming a good digital citizen."

Children need similar guidance at home, too, even though they may not realize it. Let your child know when you see him making good decisions about his use of technology. "Hey, I noticed you've been spending more time at those sites that teach you how to code. Tell me about that." When he goes off track, give him a good-natured, nonjudgmental nudge to get back to work. "You've been taking a pretty long break from your homework, watching videos. You wouldn't be procrastinating now, would you?" And if he's really off track, nip it in the bud before it becomes a habit. "Hey, I know you need to be online to do your homework, but you've been online doing everything else except homework all night. What's going on?"

- Don't assume your child knows more about technology than you do, just because he's good at apps and games. He still needs your guidance to use technology constructively.
- Do use his screentime as a cue to look for ways to guide, but not take over (unless necessary), his decisions about how he's using it.

Recognize and Use a Teachable Moment

Gracie is a fourth-grader whose mother sought me out to discuss what she saw as her daughter's increasing dependence on the use of her iPad. Gracie had been spending too much time on it and when it was time to turn it off, she'd get into fights with her parents.

I explained the meaning of voluntary and involuntary attention to Gracie's mom. Having a background in biology, she easily grasped what this meant to the development of her daughter's brain pathways. She decided to start talking with Gracie about the power that her iPad was having over her. Also, she instituted iPad holidays that her daughter halfheartedly went along with. She told me this story about their very first one.

The day was going along without a hitch until Gracie told her mom that she wanted to FaceTime with her grandparents. She made a case for how that shouldn't count the same way as other apps. Her mom agreed with her but went on to explain that once she took out her iPad to use for FaceTime, she'd be tempted to want to stay on it. Today she could call them on the phone.

Gracie grew insistent and did her best to argue her case. Her mom did not take the bait although her mind was bursting with things to say back to Gracie. For instance, the girl's grandparents lived only a few towns away and she saw them in person about once a week. Why the urgency to FaceTime with them today? But her mom held back. Instead, she continued in a spirit of agreement with her daughter. In fact, she told Gracie she was proud of her for recognizing the value of FaceTime for bringing their family together. She said it was mature of her to think of that, and it was such a good point that when she had more control over turning her iPad off without creating a scene, FaceTime would *then* qualify as an exception on iPad holidays.

Gracie continued to protest, and her mom, running out of patience, quietly gave her the choice to call on the phone or not. She then moved on to what she'd been doing before. As an afterthought, she added, "Talk it over with Grandma and Grandpa on the phone and see what they say about it." Gracie shot her mother a sharp look. "You *know* what they'll say." Gracie wasn't happy but she got the message. It was her first step in the long journey of taking responsibility for having to face hard choices about her own screentime, including the tricks she might play on herself to get more of it.

- Don't back down if your child starts to show resistance. It's a sign that she needs the structure of rules to help her.
- Do give her a face-saving way to accept what she doesn't want to hear.

Help Children Tell the Difference between Using Technology as a Tool or as a Toy

As Gracie astutely observed, not all apps are created equal. Some digital media clearly serve as tools to learn and create, some are pure entertainment, and many blur the distinction between tool and toy.

For young children, keep in mind that the iPad is always at least part-toy. Even though an app was designed as a learning tool, if your child is using it primarily to alter her mood, then in that sense, it's functioning more as a toy. Of course, you want your child to be happy, but you don't want her to forget how to find happiness without a screen to entertain her. Your child's level of resistance to turning her touchscreen off is an indicator of how dependent she's becoming on it for continuing levels of elevated stimulation.

For grade-school children, start an ongoing conversation about the merits and drawbacks of their screentime activities. If they need help to admit to the downsides, coax them the way Gracie's mom did, without arguing, threatening, nagging, or lecturing.

- Ask them what they're *not* doing, like moving their bodies or reading books.
- Commend them when they acknowledge both the minuses and the pluses of their favorite onscreen activities.
- Help them connect the dots between their good choices about screentime and achieving their goals like better grades.

The teen years are, and have always been, a time for kids to branch out and experiment with their identities and roles with friends and peer groups. Today, to a large extent, kids do this online. Your teenager is capable of understanding that while screentime helps her reach her social goals, it can also get in the way of her academics, sports, and other personal goals. When she loses sight of this, you'll need to give her a nudge.

- Keep talking with your teen about her screen activities and how her choices are helping or hurting her chances for success.
- Discuss the value of a tech holiday if she needs to reset. Take one with her to show solidarity.
- Find the sweet spot between respecting your teen's privacy and stepping in so you can protect her not-yet-fully-grown brain.

There is no substitute for putting in the time to learn more about your child's favorite screen activities so you and she together can distinguish tool from toy. Also, keep in mind, this is an exercise in awareness, not a banishing of toys.

- Don't look at all screentime the same way.
- Do teach your children to discriminate between using a screen as a tool or a toy.

Make Rules Together

You are the parent and your word is final when it comes to making rules for your children. However, a wise parent understands the benefits of children participating in the making of their own rules. For one, your child is much more likely to keep them. And, since the goal is for her to learn how to make rules for herself, making rules together is a golden learning opportunity. It's a teachable moment to help your child understand how and why we need rules about using technology.

Younger children need you to give them clear, simple rules, but you can still start early giving them some say in the matter. For example, if the rule is that they can play on their iPad until a timer goes off, give them their choice of which ringtone you'll use to set the timer. This may sound like a small thing, but think about how you feel when your alarm goes off. An alarm of your child's choosing can take the edge off a potentially irritable reaction. Better yet, create a few ringtones that make your child laugh and let her pick a different one each time. That way, learning how to stop includes a few smiles, instead of a tense game of tug-of-war between the two of you.

A word about timers . . . They're a useful first step in your child realizing it's not you stopping her fun but the reality of the way the world works. There are more things than there is time to do them, and that is true for all of us. The reason your child needs to stop is not because you're mean; it's because there's only so much time in the day. Plus, timers are useful tools because it's tougher to argue with a timer.

Most kids will adapt to timers easily if they're presented the right way—a happy sound that announces it's time to do the next thing you're going to do today. Since timers and alarms will be an important tool in your child's future, I strongly caution parents about using them as any part of a punitive measure, such as sending a child to her room to stay until a timer goes off. If using a timer has negative associations for your child, she's less likely to time her study breaks or screentime when she's older and on her own. Plus, young people don't wear wristwatches routinely anymore, so often their smartphone is their only immediate connection with time. The practice of using its alarm can make a huge difference in their ability to be on time reliably and to follow through with plans and effective time management.

If your child balks at using a timer, back off for now and try again later. You want to connect timers with good feelings at best and neutral feelings at worst. You're putting a useful tool in your child's hands when you help her make friends with timers.

When making rules with grade-school children, help them connect the dots between attention to their goals and setting limits on their screentime. For example: "If you get all As and Bs on your report card, we'll talk about adding another half hour of screentime every night. That's how we'll know you're able to stay focused on your work and your brain isn't too full of videos and chatting." Give them structured choice: "So let's see how you want to divide your five hours of playing video games this week. Is there a time when your friends are online playing, too?"

Teens need you to listen to what they think and help them discover strategies for themselves. The mom of a thirteen-year-old boy was telling me how she was sitting next to him while he was getting started on a social networking site. She was giving him suggestions for what to say when she soon realized her ideas were based on her social etiquette, not on what the kids on the site were saying and doing. She wisely decided to do more observing and less advice-giving.

Most homework assignments now depend on your child using technology, so it becomes harder to enforce rules that limit screentime. It's a challenge to monitor what your child is actually doing in front of a screen without hovering and creating tension. The more your child participates in making her own rules, the more likely she is to respect them on her own.

- Don't leave your child out of rules she needs to follow.
- Do use rule-making as a teachable moment.

Replace "No" with "Yes, after ______"

When your child asks if she can play *Minecraft* (for the hundredth time today), instead of saying "No," say "Yes, after you finish the outline for your history project." This helps to alter the dynamic of your exchange. Instead of setting the scene for an argument, you're creating a tone of agreement.

In an age-appropriate way, discuss the reasons why "business, then pleasure" is a time-honored axiom, so your child sees the wisdom in adopting it for herself. When presented this way—as a smart thing to do—the "Yes, after ______" strategy is *not* the same as using screentime as a dangling carrot. You're not sending the message that activities like studying or doing homework are undesirable and screen-time is forbidden fruit. You're sending the message that completing homework is so desirable that you want an effective plan to ensure it gets done.

Help your child recognize that, realistically, homework requires effort and that's why it's practical to do it first. It's also the reason why it's desirable—her efforts make a difference and move her closer to her goals in the real world.

Replacing "No" with "Yes, after ______" gives you a teachable moment to remind your child that you both want the same things—for her to feel good about herself and be successful in school. It also gives you the chance to talk about avoidance and procrastination, not as reprimands but as challenges we all face. For older kids who can grasp the concept, you can discuss the difference between voluntary and involuntary attention, what's happening inside their brains, and why it makes sense to go from studying to watching TV and not vice versa.

Ultimately, if you model the "Yes, after ______" rule yourself, apply it consistently with your child, and talk about it with her, she's more likely to live by it when you're not around. Years from now, competing for jobs and promotions that she needs to work for, the "Yes, after ______" rule will serve her well and she'll appreciate your having taught it to her much more than she does today.

- Don't lose sight of the fact that you and your child both want the same things.
- Do remain on common ground and good-naturedly practice "Yes, after ______."

Strive for Learning, Not Performance

To find teachable moments, you need to be present and available when they occur, but you do *not* want to be a helicopter parent. Do your best to see your level of involvement through the eyes of your children. During a parents-only intake interview, sometimes a parent makes a point of telling me, "I never nag." As sure as there are cat videos on YouTube, within moments of meeting her child, I'll hear, "My mom never stops nagging." Also, keep in mind, that if you string more than three words together with a period at the end, your teen will call it a lecture. Teachable moments are best accomplished using as few words as possible.

If you feel frustrated, ask yourself if your expectations are realistic. We're so primed for instant everything that it feels like our children should improve their habits more quickly than they do. It's useful to remember that we want their learning to endure, and that takes time.

As we discussed earlier in the chapter, performance is not the same as learning. We get faster results if we threaten kids with punishment when they make bad choices about their screentime, but what we get is their *performance*, not their *learning*. If any learning has taken place, it's learning how to improve at not getting caught.

Your goal is to communciate reasonableness and help your child make educated decisions on her own. Your levelheadedness and rationality will help her develop strategies that she'll want to use when you're not around. Patient, peaceful insistence on balance, not control battles, will result in your child learning to use technology responsibly.

Children need to be held accountable, and what happens if they break a rule can be part of the rule itself. One mom told me that she asked her four-year-old what she should do if her daughter didn't turn her iPad off when she was supposed to. "You be the mommy who wants her child to learn. What does the mommy do?" The little girl said, "Take it away and give it back to me when I'm grown up." Seeing her mom try not to laugh, she quickly added, "Or tomorrow morning."

- Don't expect instant results. Learning takes time.
- Do value teachable moments as you watch your child grow.

Every day, remind yourself of the 3 Rs of good attention—**R**unning, **R**eflecting, and **R**ethinking screentime. In the morning, think ahead to the day for opportunities to practice them. In the evening, think back on the day, and see how well you've done.

In the next chapter, we'll look at the most effective strategy to reduce the need to use screentime as escapism: make real life so rewarding, there's no need to escape.

7

Step Four
Turn Up Real-World Happiness

The world is full of a number of things,
I am sure we should all be happy as kings.
—Robert Louis Stevenson

As we saw in chapter 1 in the marshmallow test, the most successful strategy for young children to resist their urge to react to a hot stimulus was for them to direct their attention elsewhere. Redirecting attention to something else of personal interest is the top strategy for children and adults alike to resist urges to check e-mail, text right back, turn on the TV, or click on your browser—urges you may be feeling right this minute.

With such compelling modern-day marshmallows, we've got to have goals and interests with strong personal meaning so we can stand up to attention snatchers. For example, your dedication as a parent is stronger than your urge for a digital fix right now, and that's what keeps you reading this book.

Does your child's current go-to activity involve a screen? Ask her to write down or draw three things that make her feel happy and successful and don't require a screen. Then, instead of arguing when it's time for a nonscreen activity, find that list. Help her connect with her desire for those activities. She's more likely to let go of her screentime when she's thinking about other avenues to happiness and success than when she's arguing with you to stay online.

TUNE IN TO YOUR CHILD'S INTERESTS AND APTITUDES

On the night of July 20, 2007, I stood in a bookstore filled with children and parents eagerly awaiting the midnight distribution of preordered copies of *Harry Potter and the Deathly Hallows*. Many of the kids were dressed as Hogwarts students and other characters from the blockbuster series. It was an excellent photo-op, and a local TV station sent a reporter to interview the kids. "So, you really like reading these books?" he asked one youngster. "I like reading Harry Potter better than watching TV!" the little boy exclaimed. In a world of hundreds of cable channels, giant-screen TVs, and action-packed shows aimed at kids, the power of Harry Potter to turn children on to the joy of reading a 759-page book made him a wizard to me.

If your child is engaged in a lengthy novel, Harry Potter or not, notice what happens as she gets close to finishing. She'll pass up many of her usual onscreen activities in favor of finding out how her book will end. Her attention is diverted away from TV, websurfing, and posting, without an argument or bribe.

Children have widely diverse interests and aptitudes. Children are drawn to different books, different sports, different music, and different dreams about their future. What matters is that they're as personally invested and authentically motivated as the little boy in the bookstore who was 100 percent sincere when he said he'd rather read Harry Potter than watch TV.

Make it your mission to help your child identify and explore her own real-world aptitudes and interests, even if they're not your own or the ones you envisioned for her. Children are not blank slates.

They're born with genetic predispositions that make them better at some activities than others. These activities become the dopamine bicycles we discussed in chapter 2. Because they'll succeed more at activities that suit them, they'll like them better and do them more; and because they like them better and do them more, they'll continue to succeed. When a child gets dopamine on a steady, sustainable basis from real-world success, she doesn't need to overload on it from virtual world escapism.

Some children are so curious, they want to try everything they see—play a sport, dance, learn an instrument. Childhood is the time for that. Other children require patient encouragement to try new things. Compared to the safety of screentime at home, for them, exposure to the real world can feel scary.

Encourage your child to let her imagination run wild—make-believe she's an exotic animal, pretend she's traveling to outer space, play silly games, tell far-fetched stories, or make up rhymes and songs. Don't let organized activities strangle her creativity. Provide an atmosphere that emboldens your child to be original, spontaneous, and free.

ACCEPT YOUR CHILD'S UNIQUENESS

Brad's dad, a linebacker in college, slipped a Nerf football into his infant son's cradle. Robin's mother started her on violin lessons when she was three years old. Tom's parents saved all their woodworking materials from before they were married, to someday share their favorite hobby with their future children. Sometimes kids follow in their parents' footsteps and sometimes they don't.

Make peace with the fact that if they don't, they're not rejecting you. They're living their own lives. Feel good about raising children who feel free to be themselves and who trust you enough to do that.

According to conventional wisdom, parents should tell children they can achieve whatever they want. Theoretically, this sounds like a vote of confidence in your child that could only fire up his motivation. In reality, though, words like these sometimes bring about the opposite of their intended effect. Some children end up comparing themselves unfavorably to others who have natural aptitudes for popular activities. This stops them from identifying, valuing, and developing their own unique gifts. Dejected, they go home and watch TV or find relief from any screen to escape their disappointment.

This is especially true for children with attention problems. Often, they feel lacking in what it takes to succeed at school and organized clubs and sports that require concentration. Robert Brooks, a psychologist who specializes in treating ADHD, saw this in his practice every day. He described these children as "drowning in an ocean of self-perceived inadequacy." He developed the metaphor of helping children discover their "islands of competence."[1]

If your child is adrift, help him find and explore his island of competence and don't stop until you do. You probably have some sense of his natural aptitudes. If you're truly at a loss, ask him, "What are you good at?" This is a better question than, "What do you like?" which typically yields popular answers not personal ones.

Don't be discouraged if nothing seems to stick. The act of trying new things is a course of discovery that teaches your child useful skills and, at the same time, keeps him away from attention snatchers. Keep this effort framed in positive terms and protect your child from forming a habit of quitting a new activity prematurely.

By all means, encourage your child to dream big. Let him know that with hard work, the sky is the limit and there most definitely is a time and place for his star to shine.

RECOGNIZE THE NEED FOR TOO MUCH ESCAPISM

Chris, a middle-schooler, was the living definition of a kid who was falling through the cracks. He just got by with his grades in school. None of the kids disliked him, but he had no close friends. In the afternoons, he went online and watched videos and browsed new music for hours. At night, he watched TV. When his parents began to talk with him about the amount of time he spent on the Internet, he started to leave the house in the afternoons. It didn't take long for them to discover that he was going to the library to watch videos and listen to music.

Almost from the start, Chris had struggled in school. His parents wanted him to have ample time for homework so they didn't encourage lots of after-school commitments. Soon they saw that Chris wasn't interested in homework or extracurricular activities. They tried to get him involved in sports, but he shied away. He showed some interest in bodybuilding. When he traveled with his family, he'd go to the hotel gym with his dad, but the gyms around his neighborhood didn't allow children. His dad got him a set of barbells to use at home, but he'd only lift weights if he could watch TV while he did it.

Chris was evaluated for learning disabilities and the report mentioned that he might also be mildly depressed. Chris's parents were concerned and sought professional help. Chris's pediatrician referred them to a psychiatrist who discussed the use of antidepressants with them. Chris and his parents were open to the idea, but they wanted to try other approaches first.

After I spoke with Chris, it seemed to me that watching TV and surfing the web were ways that Chris was managing his own depression. He was altering his mood so as not to fall into an abyss. In a sense, he was using his screentime to self-medicate. He was trying to make himself feel better. I explained to his parents that when someone becomes dependent on anything to meet an emotional need like that, to him, it's scaffolding. It provides a secure foothold in an otherwise precarious place. You can't get someone to give up his scaffolding unless you can replace it with something else or unless the need for it no longer exists.

I encouraged Chris and his parents to talk together about his interest in videos and music. At first, he was reticient, anticipating disapproval because he liked grunge rock. His parents did their best to understand their son's music, and gradually Chris opened up about it. His parents had their limits, but they did start to listen along with Chris, at home and in the car. They put together playlists of tracks they all liked (or that Chris liked and his parents were learning to like).

Chris's parents bought him a guitar and got lessons for him, but Chris couldn't make any progress with his playing and it became a sore spot instead of a bright one.

Chris and his dad looked for concerts by bands that Chris liked. If his friends weren't interested in going, Chris's dad went with him. At the concerts, Chris's dad noticed that his son was constantly in motion, keeping the beat with his hands and feet, even more than the other kids did. Previously, he'd observed Chris at home, tapping his fingers to the music. He thought it may have been a nervous habit, but now he was seeing it in a new light.

Chris's dad bravely suggested drum lessons to his son. After feeling disappointed about his failed attempt to learn to play the guitar, Chris was ambivalent. One night, Chris's dad brought home a practice pad and some drumsticks and quietly handed them to his son. It didn't take long for Chris to download a metronome app and some lessons, and start to practice.

After a few months of private lessons from a drummer in a local band, Chris was playing with ease. He practiced daily and soon got a set of drums. He was pretty good at it by the time he entered high school. There he discovered that the school was full of ambitious guitarists, but no one could drum as well as Chris. His skill was in demand and he expanded his musical tastes and played with several different kinds of bands. TV and websurfing became a nonissue. Chris no longer had time for it. Learning how to play the drums had replaced the scaffolding that screentime had provided. Eventually, Chris's confidence in his musical skill and in making new friends made scaffolding unnecessary.

If your child is becoming dependent on electronic escapism, ask yourself what it is he needs to escape from, and look for ways to restore enthusiasm in his life. TV and video games provide social currency for kids. Social media keeps them connected around the clock. In these ways, they contribute to your child's sense of belonging in his world. Be on the lookout, though, that they don't become a poor substitute for your child taking real-world risks and reaping real-world rewards.

KEEP CHILDHOOD FREE FROM THE NEED FOR TOO MUCH ESCAPISM

One day in my office, in the midst of a conversation about her extracurricular activities, a high school junior lost her composure and snapped, "I'M SICK OF HEARING WHAT I HAVE TO DO TO GET INTO COLLEGE." Her mother was mortified and kept apologizing to me, "She's not like this. I don't know what's gotten into her." Truth be told, I've seen so many students who are so tightly wound, I was surprised it was the first time this happened.

We joke about the absurdity of toddlers being prepped for admissions interviews to get into the right preschools to continue on to the best grade schools that feed into the highest-ranked high schools that earn the most slots into Ivy League colleges. But the pressure we put on our children to compete for grades, test scores, and prestigious school admissions is no joke to them.

Their experience of their childhood often includes a background, low-level anxiety that never goes away completely. It's a reflection of our anxiety about their future in a competitive world. It's a voice that tells them: It's not enough to enjoy playing lacrosse. You need to make the varsity team because it will look good on your college application. You can't just have fun in the drama club. You have to be president and also produce a play. You can't just enjoy traveling this summer. You need to have an exciting adventure, learn a lesson from it, and take notes so you can write a standout college essay.

Kids can no longer run free outdoors on their own as they once did to blow off steam. Concerns for safety limit how much freedom we allow them to have. For many, afternoons and weekends are a series of nonstop lessons and organized activities scheduled back-to-back. Plus, as children get older, the always-on nature of social media limits their freedom to relax and be themselves. Friends expect witty and immediate responses. Smartphones have cameras so kids have to look camera-ready at all times. Inevitably, they won't, and their friends may take and post an unflattering photo or video of them. Also, if your kid had an embarrassing moment or a disagreement with her friends today at school, it no longer ends when she leaves to come home. Her friends will continue the conversation on social media. No wonder kids often want to get lost in a TV show or video game that makes them forget about the day.

Protect your child's childhood. Keep an eye on your child's stress level. Is she getting enough sleep and exercise? Becoming more irritable? Spending more time than usual in front of a screen?

Keep the lines of communication open, but be careful not to question in a way that sounds like you're interrogating. Most kids hate being asked, "How was school today?" especially in the car on the way home. Better is to offer a few kind words: "It's good to see you, honey."

Don't underestimate the nurturance you provide by being fully present for your child, not as a busy chauffeur who returns calls while getting her kid to music lessons on time but as the warm, reassuring presence that makes everything feel OK again when unbeknownst to you, your child had an incident at school today, or a bad grade on a test, or a misunderstanding with a friend.

Often, the reason kids don't tell you what's stressing them out is that they don't want parents to try to fix their problems. It's hard to refrain from immediately offering solutions when you realize your child is struggling, but consider the benefits of active listening that we discussed in Step Three (chapter 6). Your child will feel listened to and validated, more confident in her ability to think for herself, and more willing to talk with you again in the future.

Help your children manage their stress with sufficient sleep, exercise, and downtime that's restorative. Model healthy ways to handle stress yourself.

USE TECHNOLOGY TO SPARK AND SUPPORT YOUR CHILD'S INTERESTS

Whatever your child is into—sports, music, arts and crafts, fashion, cooking, you name it—there's an app for it. Websites, instructional videos, and myriad apps can bridge your child's attraction to technology with new nontech interests. Runners can map their routes and track their times. Fitness buffs can find workouts and motivating music. Book lovers can discover new titles. Chess players can practice with the greats. Future musicians can learn to play any instrument. Budding photographers, graphic artists, and filmmakers can find apps at every level from novice to pro. The Internet is endless, which is its blessing and its curse.

The challenge is to help your child use digital media to further her goals without getting sidetracked by an attention snatcher. When your child is young, you can be there, on hand, to help redirect her back to the reason she went online in the first place. But as your child gets older, close supervision of her online activity becomes less practical and often backfires. Adolescents resent it when a parent hovers over them. We'll discuss more about involvement with your teen's online activity in Step Five (chapter 8). At every age, you can help your child stay on track when she goes online by supporting her goals and continuing your efforts to strengthen her voluntary attention.

SOLVE PROBLEMS TOGETHER, ESPECIALLY IF YOUR CHILD'S INTEREST *IS* TECHNOLOGY

For years, my office was not far from Sorrento Valley in San Diego, headquarters for Qualcomm and other major telecommunication companies. San Diego is home to aerospace, biotech, computer peripheral, multimedia, and software firms. It's no surprise that many of the families I've seen in my practice include parents and children with considerable computer skills.

What I learned in my work with science-minded students—and their engineer parents—was that more often than not, they're happiest when solving problems. The most common reasons for these children to be referred to my practice were that they weren't paying attention in school or making friends easily. Not knowing how to deal with boredom had quite a bit to do with it.

When I'd work with a family, once an issue was out on the table without blame or shame or anger, it became a problem to be solved. The kids didn't necessarily like it, but they appreciated a solution that worked. For example, one youngster was having difficulty waking up in the morning as he didn't particularly look forward to certain aspects of his school day. It was becoming an ordeal to get him up and out of bed. His sister had an idea. He could set his alarm with the theme music from his favorite video game. He thought it over, decided it could work, downloaded a few bars of the theme as a ringtone, and set it as his alarm.

It wasn't a perfect solution. His parents were worried that hearing the theme first thing every morning would cause their son to want to play the game even more than he already did. His dad hoped that if it worked, eventually he'd change the ringtone to other music that he liked. They decided it was worth a shot. The young man still didn't care for getting up to go to school, but he did wake up to the new alarm and he was glad to have solved a problem that was getting him in trouble at school and making life miserable every morning for the entire family at home.

One day in my office, another young techie similarly acknowledged the beauty of a solution he didn't like. He was an incoming freshman at High Tech High, a San Diego charter school that integrates technical skills with learning. It has become a magnet school for kids who like to code for fun. Upon discovering he needed to maintain a certain grade in Spanish, this student expressed disappointment and frustration. At the same time, however, he objectively pointed out that he was a "numbers guy" and this was the only way he'd ever be motivated to study a foreign language.

If your child's main interest is programming, website design, computer animation, or any other activity that requires him to stay in front of a screen for long periods of time, he's probably already come face-to-screen with the problem of wasting time at sites that amuse him when he's bored or tired. As you read in chapter 2, when his prefrontal cortex is fried, his sensory cortex is ready for entertainment. Learning what he needs to do to protect himself from attention snatching is a problem he needs to solve, especially in view of the fact that computers are going to play a major role in his future.

Listen to his ideas and encourage him to keep generating solutions. Do what you can to help him see the value of stopping for a healthy break to reset. He's likely to know or be able to find the most highly rated productivity apps and browser extensions that clock how long he's been on a website. Some apps will ask him periodically if he really wants to stay there, allow him to set a limit for his visit before he starts, or block a site for him during his worktime. Be prepared to get some first-rate tech tips that you can use yourself.

REINFORCE YOUR CHILD'S GOALS

Think of a time when you're working toward a specific goal with a specific deadline that has meaning for you—getting ready for houseguests or packing for a vacation. You don't have time for TV or websurfing. The attentional weight of your goal is greater than the attentional weight of those attention snatchers. The same is true for your child.

If your child is going to pitch this season, play in a recital, compete in a chess match, or make honor roll, and it's a goal that has meaning to him, he'll want to practice and won't have time to let his attention get snatched. You can help your child create meaningful goals and support him in making progress toward them. You can encourage him through the ups and downs of working toward a goal.

We're all inspired when we watch the Olympics. It's a prime example of the astonishing feats we can accomplish as human beings. During the broadcast, from time to time, we see video clips of human interest stories about the athletes, which might include about a half minute of a training session. Almost all the media coverage is on an athlete's moments of glory, not his years of grueling practice. It's easy to overlook the reality of setting small, incremental goals every day in order to achieve bigger ones. Your child needs goals that keep him feeling a sense of progress—goals that are just out of reach, but not out of sight.

Sports psychologist Frank Schubert says, "The art of establishing a goal is to set it up in such a way that the task required and the rewards expected develop an irresistible power of attraction." Sounds like the design of a video game, doesn't it? There's a reason why in the United States 183 million gamers average thirteen hours per week—almost two hours per day—of play.[2]

TAKE A LESSON IN GOAL-SETTING FROM VIDEO GAME DESIGN

In video games, goals are

1. Well-defined—for instance, saving a princess or launching a bird at a pig.
2. Measurable. You receive a score.
3. Incremental. You have immediate goals that get you to the next level.
4. Feedback supported. You know the results of your actions right away.
5. Within a time frame. A clock is ticking or a jingle is playing. You move.
6. Attainable. The level of difficulty increases gradually. You experience success.
7. Not boring. The level of difficulty increases gradually. You experience challenge.
8. Emotionally safe. You can make mistakes.
9. Active. You practice.
10. Rewarding. Visual and audio stimuli provide variable surprise rewards and celebrate your success with you.

How can we apply these principles in real life to help our children form goals for themselves?

First, what matters to your child right now? Does she want to improve a grade this term? Audition for a school play? Be a better swimmer? Encourage her to be more specific in defining those goals:

"Get an A in math on my next test." "Get a speaking part in the spring production." "Swim eight laps of freestyle without stopping so I can get on the swim team."

Help her set trackable, incremental goals that are realistic yet challenging: "Master a times table every two nights." "Video myself reading the script every weekend." "Swim one lap farther every week." Help her find ways to get immediate feedback—for instance, using flashcards, a voice recorder, or a chart to mark her progress. And help her use that feedback to adjust her goals up or down, as needed, without any sense of defeat. "Good for you. Now we know it takes three nights to learn some of the times tables so well you can nail them on the test."

Once your child is invested in working toward a goal, use it the same way Odysseus used wax to fill the ears of his crew so they wouldn't hear the songs of the sirens. (A siren is a mythological creature whose song is so irresistible that listeners forget everything else and are drawn to them—an early Greek precursor of a ringtone.) The seductive sounds of sirens would lure sailors off their course and onto reefs where they'd get shipwrecked and stranded. Ask your child to write out or draw her answer to the question: "What's important to me?" Encourage her to have it on hand or have a similar touchstone visible in a strategic place, so she can stay connected to her goals and block out the call of attention snatchers *before* they start to tempt her.

Make sure your child knows that she's already won, in your book, by setting goals and going for them, so she feels emotionally safe enough to make mistakes. The personal satisfaction your child feels from achieving goals she's chosen for herself will mean more, run deeper, and last longer than the transitory elation she feels reaching a goal set by a game designer.

Enjoy exploring your child's aptitudes and interests and discovering what her dreams are made of. In the next chapter, we'll look at ways for you to guide the development of your child's voluntary attention through each of the stages in her growing years.

8

Step Five
Think Like a Child, Act Like a Parent

Tell me and I will forget. Show me and I may remember. Involve me and I will understand.

—Confucius

In the comic strip *Peanuts*, when Charlie Brown's teacher speaks, we see a cartoon bubble coming from the front of the classroom filled with "wah waah wah wah waaah wah waah wah." With a dash of humor, we're reminded of the difference between what an adult says and what a child hears. At no time is this more true than when an adult is speaking to a child as if the child had executive functions that he hasn't yet developed.

All day—working at the office, running a household, meeting with colleagues and friends—you strive to be articulate. You offer detailed instructions and explanations, generate intelligent discussion, and put forth persuasive arguments. It's natural that when you come home, you're ready to do the same things that made you successful during the day. However, your child's brain is not fully developed physically, and although your children hear your words, to them it sounds more like "wah waah wah wah waaah."

Step Five asks you to consider your child's developmental stage and think the way a child his age would think. As a parent, it's extremely beneficial for you to understand and remember what he's primed to learn at each stage, so you can make sure he masters those skills.

As we saw in chapter 3, your child's executive functions develop over time, and there's a sequence to the developmental tasks that build these brain pathways.

Inhibition (birth to six years old). In the early years, your child's developmental tasks center around *inhibition*. In other words, your child needs to learn how to soothe himself when he gets upset, resist a temper tantrum when he's angry, and stop himself from immediately acting on his emotions to get what he wants when he wants it—for instance, an iPad NOW!

Working Memory (seven to twelve years old). In the grade-school years, your child is putting together cause-and-effect relationships. He's building his *working memory* so he can benefit from the past to improve his decisions in the future. He's starting to anticipate the consequences of his actions, but for the most part his thinking is short-term and concrete.

Ability to Shift Perspectives (thirteen to eighteen years old). In the high school years, your teen is practicing abstract reasoning and the *ability to shift perspectives*. He's developing the facility to fluidly move from one mind-set to another. He can now base his decisions on self-observation and exercise metacognition, the ability to think about his own thinking.

The development of these functions overlaps at almost every age. Preschoolers comprehend many simple cause-and-effect relationships and young adults still face challenges with emotional self-regulation.

When they fall in love, they'll need to navigate the complexities of romantic relationships.

The chronological age ranges I use in this chapter are approximate and can vary quite a bit. Be guided by your child's behavior, not his chronological age. Also, keep in mind that executive functions are not the same as IQ or other measures of intelligence. Your child may be gifted in many ways and still lag in the development of some executive functions.

BIRTH TO SIX YEARS OLD

If your child is a toddler or a preschooler, she's learning how to control her impulses like the children in the marshmallow test. As she discovers ways to stay calm when she can't get what she wants, she builds strong connections between her prefrontal cortex (her thinking brain) and her limbic system (her emotional brain). These acts of self-control form the foundation for her future executive skills.

Teach Your Toddler to Calm Down

Every human begins life by crying to get what she wants. It's a primal response with strong survival value. (Just try sleeping through it!)

Over time, as your baby's needs are met, she becomes less frantic in her signals of hunger, discomfort, and loneliness. But she will get upset to get what she wants. Count on it.

Around two years of age, your child starts to develop a fascination with saying the word "no." Early childhood experts call this the threshold between the sensorimotor stage and the preoperational stage of cognitive development. The rest of us call it "the terrible twos."

During this time, your child is incapable of seeing things from different points of view. She doesn't understand that turning off the TV is a good thing no matter how eloquently you put forth this argument. To her, it's a sudden, inexplicable loss. Captivated by the screen when you turned it off, she probably experienced a sensation akin to how you'd feel if you just discovered your wallet was gone. Keeping this in mind can help you stay calm, which, in turn, helps her calm down more quickly.

How much screentime should a baby age two and under have? According to the American Academy of Pediatrics (AAP), as little as possible. Many parents understand this recommendation but have watched with amazement at how their one-year-old responds to a touchscreen. They're proud of how their babies have mastered apps and see touchscreen tablets as an enjoyable learning tool for them.

Some parents feel that the AAP recommendation is outdated and unrealistic, meant for TV screens but not iPads. It's important to remember, though, that it's based on the intensive, sequenced growth of a baby's brain during the first two years of life. As we discussed in chapter 3, a major shift is taking place from the brain's orienting network to the brain's executive network during this critical time. The AAP recommendation states: "Television and other entertainment media should be avoided for infants and children under age 2. A child's brain develops rapidly during these first years, and young children learn best by interacting with people, not screens."[1]

There are times when your baby will sit in front of a screen—when her older siblings watch TV, when you're in a restaurant or waiting area with screens on the walls, when you're in a quiet, confined public place like a plane and doing all you can to keep her sitting still and entertained. Knowing occasions like these will occur, it's worth considering an alternative to giving a one-year-old a screen if it can be avoided.

When your toddler is ready for a screen, do so intentionally, with a conservative time limit and active, rather than passive, digital media. What does it mean to give your child a screen *intentionally*? It means that you plan on it ahead of time. You make a conscious decision to do it at a specific time for a specific amount of time, rather than reacting to your toddler's cries for you to hand it over.

Giving your child a screen intentionally also means that the time she spends on a tablet is in addition to, not at the cost of, activities such as face-to-face contact with people, running and playing outside, reading, improvisational games of make-believe, and manipulating three-dimensional, tactile objects with her own hands. It requires you keep asking yourself the "What is she *not* doing now?" question.

As a parent, when your toddler is restless, frustrated, or upset, instead of giving her a screen to calm her down, rethink screentime, and see the situation for what it is: a teachable moment. Calm her with a soothing voice, a lullaby, and tactile comfort like a hug or contact with a plush blanket or stuffed animal. Give her the experience of allowing herself to be soothed, rather than distracted, and to be aware of her feelings, not have her attention grabbed by a screen that pulls her away from them.

These are the beginning steps for your child to learn how to calm herself down in the future, when she's on her own and gets upset at school. Each time she calms down now without depending on an attention-snatching screen, she forms essential brain pathways that are the building blocks she needs to soothe herself when you're not there and she feels let down or angry.

Understand What Your Preschooler's Behavior Is Telling You

By age four or five, your preschooler is verbally capable, except when she's upset. Then, her emotional brain takes over, and she's no longer able to use her words in a constructive way. In his groundbreaking book *Emotional Intelligence,* Daniel Goleman calls this "an amygdala takeover."[2] In other words, the older emotional limbic system seizes control of your child's brain operations.

Your preschooler's temper tantrum says, "Pay attention to me. I'm mad!" But listen also for another message, "Help! I don't know how to get back in control of my own emotions." Instead of allowing your child's anger to incite your own, step back and quietly consider the hostile takeover going on inside her brain. In this moment, the thinking part of your child's brain is powerless, a hostage to her amygdala. She needs to learn how to manage and also prevent these takeovers. The moment her amygdala lets go, you've got a teachable moment.

Stay calm until the takeover passes, being careful not to reward it, especially with an iPad. Then, when your child's thinking brain finally becomes accessible again, ask her to use her words. Reward even her smallest effort with your notice. Say, "I can see how hard you're trying to make a good choice right now," even if she still hasn't fully regained her composure.

When your child throws a tantrum and then returns to normal, no one wants to disturb the peace and rock the boat again. Giving your child the tools she needs to deal with an amygdala takeover is a lot like fixing a leaky roof. During a storm, you can't do it. But when it's sunny outside, who feels like working on the roof? You want to enjoy the good weather and believe that maybe it won't rain again.

Sure as rain, if your preschooler doesn't start practicing how to control her impulses, she'll continue extreme behaviors. When she's calm, fix the roof while the sun shines. For example, sit down and draw pictures together of things she can do when she gets upset and needs to calm herself down. She can stop and count to ten, or take three deep breaths, or sing a favorite song. Give her lots of attention and praise for her efforts to think up these good choices and get them down on paper.

Help your child learn to tell you, not show you, that she's mad. Ask, "What words can you use to tell me you don't want to turn your iPad off?" For preschoolers with an aptitude for verbal skills, a simple reminder to "use your words" can go a long way. Sometimes it helps to validate your preschooler's feelings first: "It's OK to be unhappy about that. This is a good time to use your words."

When you acknowledge your child's feelings, you reduce her need for acting out how she feels. At the same time, you're helping her build the vocabulary she needs to name her own feelings. This reduces the power that her emotional brain can have over her thinking brain. Try saying something like this: "You're mad because you want to keep playing on your iPad and it's hard to say good-bye to it for now." As soon as possible, redirect her to an attractive nonscreen activity.

Sometimes, children need more clues to connect the dots between the message their behavior is sending and the words they need to start using. When your child acts out her displeasure, give her more information to go by: "I can see you're angry. You're raising your voice and you won't look at me." If your child has a favorite character from a book or TV show, refer to a specific time when the character was angry. If Jim Henson was alive and creating Muppets today, Sesame Street might have an iPad Monster.

Keep the pictures your child drew of how to calm down on hand. Depending on your child's temperament, you may also want to have a "calm down corner"—her own personal space for solace. Remember though, using a "safe spot" is a strategy to help your child learn self-control, not a punishment because she hasn't yet learned it well enough. Its purpose is to help her discover what she needs to do, on her own, to calm down. Depending on your child's individual needs, put some books, stuffed animals, and drawing materials there. Send her there calmly, not in anger. And help her learn to send herself there when she needs it. At this stage in her cognitive development, she needs to learn inhibition.

When you think like a preschooler, keep in mind, you live in the present moment. As soon as you're free from the grip of an amygdala takeover, your thinking brain will latch on to a new challenge quickly. When you act like a parent, you'll have a change of scenery or new activity ready and waiting for your child. As she gets better at remaining calm, you can help her practice the strategy that the preschoolers in the marshmallow test used so effectively—namely, thinking about something else on her own without your help.

Make it a habit to tell your preschooler what she'll be doing after screentime *before* she begins to play on her tablet. Planting this seed early will help her be mentally prepared when the time comes to make the transition. Introduce the next activity immediately. Make the new beginning part of the old ending. Instead of saying, "It's time to put your iPad away," say, "It's time to ______, so put your iPad away." As your child gets accustomed to making the transition, say only, "It's time do this ______," and let your child put the iPad away without your instruction. Try having a touchstone for the next activity or the activity itself at hand. For example, have your jackets ready to go outside where your child can see and reach them or place a book of pictures and some tracing paper on the table right next to her.

Be creative and try out different approaches to see what works best for your child to move on to the next activity. For example, to ease a transition, some children are more drawn to activities that they've already begun, such as a picture puzzle that's partially complete. Others prefer structured choice. "Do you want your play dough or your stickers or your colored pencils?" A nudge can help. "Let's sharpen all your pencils!" At first, you may need to stick around a few minutes. "Here. I'll draw with you." Getting started is the hardest part and soon your child will be engaged on her own. If you plan for your child to have iPad time while you get a meal ready, you'll have your child's hunger working in your favor, so she leaves her iPad for dinner. (Plus you're less likely to hear a litany of "Is dinner ready yet?")

When your child loses her temper, it's natural, as a parent, to want to react immediately and fix it. Our first impulse is to threaten a punishment, "Stop that or you're in time out!" Acting like a parent means understanding that what your child needs, more than you trying to control her outburst right now, is to learn how to gain control over her own outburst. She needs to discover what works for her and practice it each time she starts to get upset so she can build and strengthen the brain pathways that support inhibition and self-control.

Use Technology to Assist You

Today's tablets and smartphones have parental controls, often called "restrictions," built right into their settings. If you're unfamiliar with the settings on your device, run a search on your operating system and read up on them or find a tech-savvy parent and make a new friend.

Take the time to set these controls before putting a device into your preschooler's hands. Also, make certain that you do the same for common websites such as safe-search filtering for YouTube and user age for Netflix. Restrict what your preschooler can access and the amount of time she can access it.

Consider getting a timelock app that disables your device after the period of time you specify. The device becomes the villain, not you, plus it eliminates nagging or having to turn the device off yourself if your preschooler is ignoring you.

When your child is this young, you have a window of opportunity for a timelock app that you won't have again. She cannot yet figure out how to cancel the timelock and so she's got to adapt to the device turning off. This is exactly the developmental task she needs to master at this age—discovering her own way to accept not getting everything she wants. With the aid of an app like a timelock, you're positioned not as the enemy but as an ally who can help her figure out how to accept the reality of "No, not now."

When she's a little older and this skill is in place, your preschooler will be in a better position to turn the iPad off herself. A good way to make this transition is by using a timer that has a tone that is friendly but seems like an outside authority. One mom I know sets her smartphone timer with a ringtone of a duck quacking. When it's time for her preschooler to turn off his iPad, it's because the duck said so and the child complies.

Even with a timelock or a timer, use iPads intentionally throughout the day like other materials. As we discussed in Step One (chapter 4), protect your child from a future of running to an iPad when no one's looking by refraining from using it as a forbidden, high-stakes reward. Also, be sure to have attractive nonscreen materials front and center as soon as the timelock has disabled your child's iPad.

Use Metacognition Because Your Preschooler Cannot

When you think like a preschooler, what's in front of you at the moment pretty much fills your world, until it doesn't. Then your world is about wandering until a new object of interest appears. Your thinking is concrete. Your brain is not yet physically capable of metacognition—thinking about your own thinking.

That's why, as a parent, you need to do your preschooler's metacognitive questioning for her. It probably won't occur to her that she's been sedentary all afternoon and she'd benefit from going outside to play. Her body might show signs of restlessness and her voice suggests she's getting irritable, but it's up to you to ask the "What is she *not* doing now?" question for her.

Asking a metacognitive question does not imply that your child should be doing one activity *or* the other. Your goal is to balance your child's use of technology. The secret to balance is to replace the word "or" with the word "and" in your thinking.

For example, the question is not should your four-year-old learn to draw from creative apps on her iPad *or* from playing with crayons, markers, and paint. Your four-year-old will learn best from ingenious art apps *and* from playing with various art media. To keep this balance, you need to stay aware of how long your four-year-old has been playing on her iPad and how dependent she's becoming on it. The fuss she puts up when it's time to turn it off is a pretty good indicator of that. Also, be sure to keep attractive art materials as accessible as the iPad.

Because the nonscreen activity calls for more voluntary attention than the screentime activity, it requires more effort and your child may resist initially. But soon momentum will kick in. If your child has already become dependent on her iPad, you may need to come up with more resourceful approaches—for instance, actively participate with her, invite friends, or choose a project with personal meaning such as letting her paint a mural in her room.

SEVEN TO TWELVE YEARS OLD

Around the time your child reaches his seventh birthday, he arrives at what is sometimes called "the age of reason." He still has work to do to control his impulses—don't we all?—but he's become better able to make cause-and-effect connections. His developmental task now is to build his *working memory,* so he can benefit from the past when he makes decisions about the future. In other words, he's learning to predict what will happen as the result of a good choice or a bad one.

His thinking is still primarily concrete, so when he connects the dots, it's between now and a specific, short-term result. For example, it's best to link his choice to turn off his device with his ability to get his homework done tonight. It's still inspiring for him to know his education will lead to his success in the future and to bring him to "take your child to work day." He's at an age of hopes and dreams. But what motivates him to concentrate on a difficult homework problem, right now, has more to do with his knowing you see and feel proud of his immediate efforts, his teacher will recognize his hard work tomorrow, and you'll take him out for a frozen yogurt when he's done.

Teach Personal Responsibility to Your Grade-Schooler

When your child was a preschooler, you probably relied on the strength of his relationship with you to get him to do certain things. For example, you might have said things like, "Mommy really wants you to taste this. You'll make me so happy." As successful as this strategy may have been, the time has come to adopt a new one.

As your child enters grade school, you begin the long journey of helping him do things because they're the right choices for him to make. When he sits at his desk in school, you're out of the picture. At his age, with his concrete thinking, this means that you're barely an influence as compared with the sights and sounds that immediately surround him, especially the distraction of other kids. Your child now needs an inner compass to make good choices about his attention.

If you're a parent who's been a natural at caring for your very young child, his transition to grade school and taking responsibility for himself may not be easy. In my practice, I've found that the parents who need to work hardest at letting go are usually those who've been the best at parenting their small child, anticipating his needs and gently guiding him as he learned to walk and talk.

One clue that can help you as a parent is to listen to the pronouns that you use. For example, when you ask your child to do something like turn off his device, do you say, "I need you to turn off your iPad"? When it's time to start his homework, do you say "Let's start your homework"? If you do, chances are that you haven't yet updated the way you think about your child, who is now capable of assuming responsibility himself for shutting off his device or starting his homework.

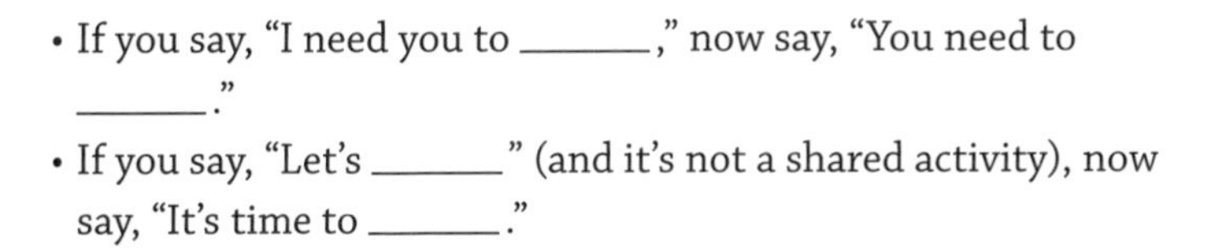

- If you say, "I need you to ______," now say, "You need to ______."
- If you say, "Let's ______" (and it's not a shared activity), now say, "It's time to ______."

This may sound like an insignificant difference, but choosing the correct pronouns helps to create the right mind-set for you and your child. It clarifies who's responsible for your child's choices and actions.

In the primary grades, you may need to remind yourself that homework is your child's responsibility. Help him only if he needs and appreciates it. If your companionship helps to settle him down, do your own deskwork or read a book sitting next to him. If he feels discouraged, provide moral support. But ultimately, homework belongs to your child. Many times, it will seem kinder and be easier to do parts of your child's homework for him, especially if your child is overwhelmed. You'll soon discover that the more you do for him, the less he does for himself.

When it comes to homework, children benefit enormously from structure. Give young children a specific time and place for homework. As they get older, give them structured choice: for example, "In order to be done with your homework before dinner tonight, by what time do you need to start?" Or, "Do you want to begin with your math or with your history assignment right now?"

To make structured choice work, be careful of your tone of voice. Try this exercise. Silently repeat this example three times, using a different intonation each time: (1) sarcasm, (2) threat, and (3) kindness. Say "It's 8 P.M. Are you going to turn off the TV on your own, or could you use a little help doing that?" Consider the different ways your child will hear it, and the different responses each tone of voice draws.

Young children want you to see them as grown-up and capable, and you can use that to your advantage. Say, "It's 8 P.M. Are you mature enough to turn off the TV by yourself?" And after your child has done it, say, "That was very responsible of you."

Understand What Your Grade-Schooler's Behavior Is Telling You

Many parents today are baffled by their children's behavior. They're good kids, so why do they waste their time and procrastinate as they do? It's a natural temptation to compare our kids to ourselves at the same age they are now and see them as less motivated to buckle down. But none of us knew how to work a smartphone before we were potty-trained. Our children's brains are forming in response to higher rates of stimulation than our brains did, giving them great potential for using technology—once they harness the power of their own attention.

Some parents feel a sense of resignation. They see their kids doing what all the other kids are doing—watching TV and texting while they do their homework and putting off assignments until the last minute. "It's the age," they say. But it's up to us to remember that children's brains are not fully grown and ours are. Acting like a parent means watching over the formation of our children's habits of attention.

Many of the children I see in my practice describe having "attention swings." Either they're really excited about something or they're really bored. It's hard for them to achieve goals that require sustained attention. They don't believe it's possible for them to achieve a goal like "get a better grade." They don't know how to break up a big goal into smaller goals and find ways to keep meeting those smaller goals over time. In other words, they need structure and support, but they don't know that. All they know is that they're expected to do something they believe they can't do and they find relief when they escape into a screen.

In my book *Find Your Focus Zone,*[3] I describe the upside-down U-curve that represents the relationship between stimulation and voluntary attention. Stimulation increases your ability to exercise voluntary attention, but only up to a point. After that, you become overstimulated and start to lose your ability to concentrate on your own.

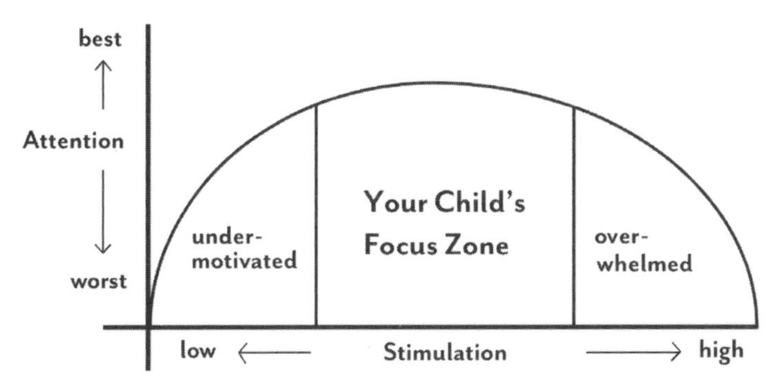

Your Child's Focus Zone on the Upside-Down U-Curve

When children have attention swings they go from being understimulated to being overstimulated without spending much time in the middle part of the curve, where sustained attention is at its best. And as parents, we can easily mistake which side of the curve they're on, especially when it's homework time.

We assume that kids are dawdling and spending time on their digital devices because they're on the left-hand side of the curve, understimulated and undermotivated. What's often the case, though, is that they don't know how to start. They're scared because they can't do what's expected of them. They're afraid of failing, making a mistake, being graded poorly, not doing as well as their classmates, or disappointing parents, teachers, or themselves. In other words, they feel too much pressure. They're actually on the right-hand side.

As a parent who thinks his child is not taking homework seriously enough, you're likely to start to apply pressure to try to get your child motivated to start his work: "If you don't get your homework done right now, you're grounded." But what's really happening is that your child is overwhelmed and anxious, avoiding because he doesn't believe he can do what's expected. The added pressure results in a meltdown.

By this time, it's too late at night for your child to do his homework. He's miserable. You're frustrated. You're stuck with the choice to either let him fail the assignment or write a note explaining he couldn't complete it due to personal or family reasons.

What needs to happen is for you to recognize early on that your child needs help. Calmly sit down and give him the structure and support he needs to get into his focus zone and complete his assignment. This doesn't happen as the result of one homework session. It's the result of many patient repetitions. This is the foundation for your child to break the habit of attention swings and build good study habits that strengthen his working memory, which is the developmental task for his age.

REWARD ATTENTION, NOT INTERRUPTION

"I see Ryan is listening. And so is Amy. And so are Sam and Peter." "I see table three is ready to go. And now table one is, too." Classroom teachers know that it's more effective to single out the kids who are paying attention than the ones who aren't. Attention from authority is rewarding and we want to reward desirable behaviors because children will repeat the behaviors we reward.

It's much harder to do this at home with children, because when a child is focused on reading or doing homework, we don't want to distract him by giving him our attention. Because of this, children usually do their homework until they get stuck on a problem and need help. Then they stop and get out of their seats to go get a parent to help them with it.

Unfortunately, this design rewards stopping, not sustained attention. Of course, when a child is studying and he's got momentum, there's a certain amount of inherent reward in the flow of his learning and the progress he's making. But children benefit from noninterruptive rewards that acknowledge the effort they're making to exercise voluntary attention over lengthy periods of time.

Noninterruptive rewards are a chance for you to be creative and apply the knowledge you have of what makes your child happy without distracting him. For example, if you see him making a real effort to stay on task, slip him a note or a happy face, or bring him a lemonade and a cookie. As soon as possible after he's finished, let him know how proud you are of how long he worked on his homework. Emphasize his effort, especially when he doesn't allow himself to lose interest and get distracted. Let him know that you notice. Make a new rule: the quiet wheel gets the grease.

Help Your Grade-Schooler Connect the Dots

Jan, a gregarious fourth-grader, was a walking pop-culture encyclopedia. She watched TMZ, knew the latest celebrity gossip, and enjoyed sharing links to videos that were going viral. She was pleasant at home and popular at school. She was getting mostly Bs on her report cards, but when she was in the primary grades, Jan had showed a lot more promise. Jan's parents said she was reading before she entered kindergarten.

Jan did just enough to get by. Her teacher could tell that she was smart but wasn't applying herself. Jan read magazines and articles online, but would only read a book if she had to for school. Her parents could see she was happy and didn't want to pressure her. At the same time, they were concerned. She was getting into the habit of not expecting a lot from herself.

Repeatedly, Jan's parents talked with her about what it takes to get into a good college, but that didn't make any difference. Then, during the summer before fifth grade, they began to collect infomation about the middle school where Jan was headed the following year. They learned how Jan could take classes like prealgebra if she entered the school with better grades. They began to talk with Jan about being stuck in slower classes when she got there.

Being a bright kid, Jan started to ask around and talk to her friends' older siblings. She realized her parents were right. Together, they made new rules for the coming school year that included tech-free time. Occasionally, in the evenings, they walked around the middle-school campus. Jan went to a play there with her friends and kept the program on the bulletin board in her room as a touchstone to remind her this year would be different. And it was.

Preteens like Jan are at an age of rich potential, but they're still concrete thinkers. They're old enough to understand cause and effect yet limited in its application to their lives. At this stage, they need your help with decisions and rules even if they don't realize it themselves.

Link Responsibility and Freedom for Your Child

The American Academy of Pediatrics (AAP) warns parents that "studies have shown that excessive media use can lead to attention problems." Some of these studies are discussed throughout this book and include both active media such as video games and passive media such as TV. (A number of these studies are discussed in chapter 11.) The AAP recommends the following: "Children and teens should engage with entertainment media for no more than one to two hours per day, and that should be high-quality content. It is important for kids to spend time on outdoor play, reading, hobbies, and using their imagination in free play."[4]

The AAP encourages parents to provide nonelectronic formats such as books and board games and, when children do use electronic media, the AAP suggests that parents participate so they can guide their children's media experience. For example, they encourage parents to watch TV with their kids to put content into context and constructively contribute to their children's media literacy. They recommend parental supervision: "To help kids make wise media choices, parents should monitor their media diet."

Grade school is the ideal time for parents to be actively involved in their children's use of electronic media. Children's media habits are still highly formative. Plus, in a few short years, privacy issues will become a hot topic in your home as your teen seeks greater autonomy and needs more of his own space.

Now is the time for you to talk with your child about how he uses his screentime and discuss what a savvy consumer of electronic media needs to know. Just as you watch TV with your child, go online with him, too. Get to know the sites that he and his friends like to frequent. Watch some of his favorite YouTube videos. Play the games he plays, with or without him, to get a sense of what he's doing and appreciate the benefits these games have to offer. Get a picture of what kinds of media attract him and why. When you and he talk about his media choices, you'll be able to relate to what he's saying and speak from a place of understanding.

Another reason to keep a close eye on your child's media experience is for you to assess how much freedom of choice he can handle. Some kids make faster progress at good decision-making than others. Each child has his own temperament and timetable for maturity and self-discipline.

Like many others in my field, I'm often asked the question, "At what age is my child ready for ______?" For the last several years, that blank was often the word "Facebook." Lately, it's also "Instagram," "Twitter," "Vine," "WhatsApp," or the networking sites du jour with teens and preteens. Like most questions about your child's maturity, the answer is "it depends."

Norms and rules about online activity change rapidly. At this time, the Children's Online Privacy Protection Act (COPPA) prohibits websites that collect information about users, such as Facebook, from registering anyone under thirteen years of age without verifiable parental consent. Most websites comply by stating that registrants must be at least thirteen years of age. However, a major nationwide survey in 2012 by *Consumer Reports* revealed that in the United States, 5.6 million kids under the age of thirteen (or 3.5 percent of the country's Facebook users) have accounts.[5] They also found that the least vigilant parents were those of children aged eleven to thirteen.

Facebook is currently working on a way to obtain verifiable parental consent so kids under age thirteen can join. But it's not rocket science for underaged kids to sign up for any networking site now. They just need to figure out a new year of birth and enter it at registration.

Many register with their parents' knowledge. Another survey taken at about the same time showed that 55 percent of parents of twelve-year-olds said their child was on Facebook and 76 perent of those parents said they'd helped their child sign on.[6] The *Consumer Reports* survey reported that the majority of parents who knew their underage child was on Facebook had not discussed the responsible use of Facebook with them, and approximately one-third did nothing to keep up with their underage child's Facebook activities.

If you've had a good attitude and been involved with your child's use of digital media all along, it will feel natural to start talking with him about social networking sites now. If you haven't had these conversations before now, it's not too late to start. For most parents, the first issues that come to mind are safety and privacy in public spaces, but it's also important to talk with your child about the impact of screentime on his attention. Screentime will invariably increase once your child signs up for social media. You may be pleasantly surprised at how well your child will respond to your interest and guidance, if you approach it in a respectful, caring, and careful way.

Think of it like this. If you visit a foreign country or a busy city, your child wants your guidance and protection. What he doesn't want is to feel embarrassed. At a certain age, you stop holding his hand in public, but you still look out for him and he's glad that you do.

At one time, TV and computer screens could be limited to communal spaces, such as the family room. Now, handheld devices provide TV and online content anywhere, anytime, seen only by your child's eyes. Apps such as Snapchat erase pictures and messages within ten seconds, which prevents parental monitoring—the main reason kids use it. (It's common for kids to believe that when their snaps disappear, they're totally irretrievable, which is not entirely true.)

Talk with your growing child about the link between responsibility and freedom. One way he can show you he's ready for greater freedom is by making the "Yes, after ____" rule his own. Another is by his willingness to be honest and respectful with you and appreciate your honesty and respect for him when the two of you discuss his online activities. With freedom, comes responsibility and in the immortal words of Abraham Lincoln, "You cannot escape the responsibility of tomorrow by evading it today."

Ask Metacognitive Questions with Your Grade-Schooler

Around this age, children are beginning to develop the capacity to ask the "What am I *not* doing now?" question, and answer it in concrete terms. As a parent, you want to help your grade-schooler along with that process. When left on his own, if your child is engaged with a screen, he's unlikely to reflect on the fact that he's been sedentary all day, neglecting the importance of physical activity. You can plant those seeds by telling him about the ability he has to take a step back and observe himself, as if he was someone else looking on.

A good way to introduce this metacognitive question is as an exercise of imagination, picturing what a specific person would say if he saw your child at that moment. For example, if your child has been marathon-watching *Big Bang Theory* all afternoon, ask, "If Coach ______ saw you on the couch glued to the TV like this, what do you think he'd say?"

It's still up to you, as a parent, to do most of the metacognitive thinking for your grade-school child—for example weighing the pros and cons of how much time he spends playing video games. (More on video games later in this chapter, and also in chapters 9 and 11.) Video games teach useful skills to your child and provide social currency for him to make and keep friends. However, gaming can quickly take up more time than your child can afford to give to it, especially if he has a natural affinity for it. If you aren't already doing so, familiarize yourself with the games that he plays.

We'll discuss the merits of multigenerational gaming in Step Six (chapter 10). If you don't already play video games with your child, start now, while he's happy you want to play with him. If you like games, it'll be easy. If you need to warm up to them, start simple—for example, with a game that keeps you physically active when you play. These include sports, workout, or dance games, such as *Just Dance*. Another starter type of game you can easily play together is a racing game, such as *Mario Kart*. It's best to choose your child's favorite games to play with him. Don't worry if the rules seem complicated at first. You've got a personal instructor who'll be delighted to teach you. There's nothing a child likes better than telling his parent what to do.

If your child is spending too much time playing video games, it's important that he not feel ashamed of this or he'll try to hide it from you. Instead, let him know that you're starting to understand why it's so hard for him to stop. From time to time, check in with him about it and generate helpful ideas together. When both of you are playing, introduce the use of a timer. If your child balks at the thought of a timer, call it a "reverse alarm" because it signals "stop" instead of wake up and start the day. Discuss the value of anticipating ahead of time that it will be hard to quit when the alarm goes off. It will help him to be prepared for that moment. Suggest a plan, such as having the next thing to do ready and waiting or at least forming a clear picture of it in his head.

When your child is playing on his own and he uses a timer or any similar strategy, let him know that you're proud of the way he's developing awareness and self-control. If he's having trouble stopping when the alarm goes off, refer back to your earlier conversations about being prepared for it. If you create the right conditions, this is a useful teachable moment, not a reason to argue or fight.

THIRTEEN TO EIGHTEEN YEARS OLD

As your child enters her teenage years, her executive functioning is now maturing, although "maturity" may not be the first word that comes to a parent's mind to describe his teen. Your adolescent's developmental task is to build brain connections that strengthen her *ability to shift perpectives.* Her thinking can now move from concrete to abstract, from immediate to long-term, from what-I-think to what-you-think. In adolescence, your child develops the capacity for abstract reasoning, including metacognition—the ability to think about her own thinking.

Understand Your Teenager's Brain

Do you remember when you were a teen and the risks you took back then? When I pose this question to parents of teens, I usually hear something like, "Of course I do. Why do you think I'm so worried about her now?"

Scientists have confirmed that the teen brain is built for risk-taking, especially when it comes to peer relations. It's an adaptive feature, both for the teen who needs to leave a safe home and move into unfamiliar territory and for the species who needs its young to mate, master new environments, and spread out across the globe.[7]

Adolescents weigh risk versus reward differently than adults do. When they link a risk to the promise of a reward, their brains give the anticipated reward greater weight than an adult brain does. The brain chemical dopamine primes and fires their reward circuits more intensely, which overpowers concerns about costly or dangerous outcomes. At this stage in their development, they tend to be emotionally reactive and can be prone to amygdala takeovers. They're capable of extremely brave feats and extremely stupid ones.

Adolescents also give greater weight to social connections than adults do. Hormones and brain chemistry cause adolescents to gravitate toward other adolescents, and once in each other's orbits, that gravity is a force to be reckoned with. In addition to dopamine, which creates a magnetism for meeting new kids, nature also attunes the teenage brain to oxytocin, a brain chemical that makes social connection even more rewarding.

Teen brains, designed by nature to go out into the world, today go out into cyberspace instead. Of course, parents worry. Popular media carry stories about online predators and similar dangers. But at the same time, media has been educating us. We're now aware of cyberstalking and also catfishing—when someone pretends to be someone they're not, using social media to create a false identity. Teens are becoming more savvy about these dangers. Many now realize that questionable posts can cost them job opportunities later.

You can use media stories to help start conversations with your teens about these issues and their habits online. When you do, ask them what they think about the impact of technology on attention. Just bringing up the topic raises awareness.

Keep an Eye on Your Teenager's Habits as They're Forming

Because teen brains anticipate rewards with greater weight than adult brains do, they're more vulnerable to experimenting with substances and behaviors that reward them immediately.[8] When you think like a teen, you feel an enormous pull to spend all the time you can on social media and video games. The more time you and your friends spend online, the more normal it feels to you.

Currently an estimated 97 percent of U.S. teens play video games.[9] Without limits, a gaming habit can get out of hand. According to industry reports in 2011 for the United States, 5 million extreme gamers played an average of forty-five hours per week.[10]

How do 5 million gamers get to the point where they play longer than the equivalent of a full-time job? If you've ever gained weight, you know the answer to that question. You start by eating a few extra crackers every afternoon when you're tired. Then you add a cookie or two with your coffee. No big deal, but it sneaks up on you. You're on a trajectory to gain weight, and the sooner you stop, the better. The number of hours your teen spends online can also creep up gradually. (We'll talk more about the habit-forming aspects of video gaming in chapter 11.)

What is the maximum number of hours that a teen can spend using digital media? As previously mentioned, the American Academy of Pediatrics recommends no more than one to two hours of total screen-time per day. How much of that time can be gaming? Research on video game playing and attention for schoolwork suggests no more than one hour per weekday of gaming with reasonable playing time on the weekends,[11] or one hour per day of gaming if your child has ADHD.[12] You'll learn more about these studies in chapter 11.

It's possible you've seen it reported that research supports twenty-one hours per week of video gaming as an upper limit without detrimental effects. This report has shown up in books and articles online, some aimed at parents, but it applies to an unusually specific circumstance and lacks generalizability. It's based on research that was conducted by the military on what soldiers did when they were off-duty in Afghanistan. Findings showed that deployed troops could surf the net and play video games for twenty-one hours per week before they started to report psychological problems.[13] It's an informative study for the military but does not apply to the vast majority of people. It most especially doesn't apply to children in school.

In addition to the impact of excessive gaming on the development of voluntary action, the time it takes away from other activities is a factor. The military study, by the way, also looked at the effects of any amount of off-duty physical exercise and found it to be superior as a recreational activity. The more that soldiers engaged in physical exercise, the fewer psychological problems they reported.

Students who are serious about getting into college and entering a profession don't have three hours per day to spend on digital media that's unrelated to their schoolwork, extracurricula, or career path. But the built-in bias of a teen's brain can cause him to overlook an immediate risk, no less a gradual one. It's up to you, as the parent of a teen, to keep an eye on the trajectory of your adolescent's online behavior and offer guidance, as needed.

Be a Good Listener, but Not a Doormat

Max was a socially awkward middle-schooler who had also been a socially awkward grade-schooler. For years, Max's mom had given her son many useful suggestions on how to make friends and get along with other kids. Now in eighth grade, Max had begun to avoid her when he thought she wanted to talk to him about his social life at school. She wondered what was going on and began to worry. She asked me if I had any ideas.

I suggested to Max's mom that instead of asking her son a question about his day at school, she ask him if he wanted to talk to her about what was going on between the two of them. I encouraged her to be honest with Max about noticing that he was avoiding her. Hopefully, Max would be honest with her, too. More than likely, it would give him the chance to let her know that he'd like more privacy now. Then she could let Max know that she understood and was there if he needed her.

"But after I tell him that it seems like he's been avoiding me, what do I say to him?" she asked.

"How about, 'Do you want to talk about that?'" I replied.

"But if I say, 'I want to talk with you about that,' he'll say 'no,'" she objected.

"Did you hear what you just said?" I asked, hoping she'd noticed the way that she had turned the pronouns around. I'd suggested that she ask Max, "Do *you* want to talk about that?" She heard it the way she'd been talking to Max for years: "*I* want to talk with you about that." In different circumstances, this might be an inconsequential grammatical mix-up, but here, it spoke to the core of the problem.

Listening to our teens about their digital habits is especially important in preventing tension and fights over simple misunderstandings. Teens tend to text more freely in each other's company than adults do in adult company. Usually, they don't mean to be rude when they text in front of you while you're saying something important. They're doing what they do without seeing it through your eyes. Since the ability to shift perspectives fluidly is their developmental task at this age, this is a teachable moment. Use it to start an honest yet nonjudgmental conversation with your teen about it.

Teens can be obstinate. Do your best to listen more than you talk. Listening doesn't mean you allow your teen to walk all over you. It means that before you jump in to correct her, especially in front of others, you put yourself in her place. Reach back to the days when you had a teen brain and now imagine what it's like to live in an age with a teen brain in your head and technology in your hands.

A few years ago, an article in the business section of the *New York Times* made the rounds online because it introduced parents to some aspects of the teen culture of texting and also because it had a snappy title: "Text Generation Gap: U R 2 Old (JK)."[14] It explained how teens like to hide from their parents in plain sight and use text phrases such as "prw" (parents are watching), "pos" (parents over shoulder), or "kpc" (keep parents clueless). Parents who thought they had good relationships with their teens started to suspect their kids were deceiving them. They wondered why their kids would feel the need to do this.

I encouraged these parents to use the article as a springboard for a casual conversation with their child, keeping in mind that part of a teen's job description is to fit in socially, avoid embarassment at all costs, and prove to themselves that they don't need their parents. If you and your child share a bond of trust and you ask her about her use of "prw," you'll probably discover she's just doing it to fit in. If it hurts your feelings, let her know. Talk it through together. If your bond of trust with your teen is too weak to have this kind of conversation, then building and strengthening it is your number-one priority.

The article on teen texting led off with a real-life scenario that described a Disney executive driving his fourteen-year-old daughter and her friend to a play. As they sat in the back seat together, the girls were talking about a movie star, and the dad made a comment about him. His daughter rolled her eyes and the two girls stopped talking. In the rearview mirror, the dad saw his daughter texting and commented that it was rude to do this when she was with her friend. His daughter rolled her eyes again. "But, Dad, we're texting each other," she replied. "I don't want you to hear what I'm saying."

What would you do as the parent?

a. Stop the car and not start it again until your daughter apologizes
b. Apologize for butting in
c. Nothing
d. None of the above

Choice (a) is your fantasy response. It's satisfying to think about it but best kept to yourself. Choice (b) is your daughter's fantasy response. Choice (c) is partially correct. In the moment, it's a good idea to bite your tongue and not embarrass your daughter any further. However, at the earliest opportunity that you and your daughter can speak privately, it's time to revisit what happened.

Choosing (d) then: what do you do *after* you've driven your daughter's friend home, either that night if it's still early enough or the next morning? First, tell her what you want to talk about so she doesn't feel ambushed. "About what happened in the car on the way to the play. I'm sorry I corrected you about texting in front of your friend." Then, pause long enough to give her the chance to apologize to you for how she behaved, and maybe even explain that she did it because she didn't want her friend to think she was a wuss.

If no apology from your daughter is forthcoming, help her along by asking her to put herself in your place. Then, be quiet and listen. Don't be tempted to fill in the silence. No matter how eloquent you are, she'll probably hear "wah, waah wah, wah, waah." She needs to do the mental work of shifting perspectives here—to make the effort to see things through your eyes. If the two of you were at the gym, and you exercised for her, would her muscles get stronger? Give her the chance to realistically consider what it's like to be doing someone else a favor like driving them around and then be treated that way. Listen with calmness and recognition of her effort. If she still needs more coaching, say, "I know you appreciate my having driven you tonight, honey. It's still nice to hear the word 'thanks.'" Maybe she'll text it to you.

Teens can be emotionally reactive. That's why, as parents, we often feel reluctant to bring up subjects that could rock the boat. However, as long as we stay calm and keep an even keel, we need to speak up so our teens can learn.

Protect Your Teenager's Sleep

Does your teen sleep with her smartphone next to her bed so she can use it as an alarm to wake her up in the morning? How often does it wake her up during the night even if it's on vibrate? What's the last thing your teen does before going to sleep?

The quality of everyone's daytime attention depends on their sleep the night before, but no one ignores the harmful effects of poor sleep more than teens. For them, not missing an important text ranks higher than uninterrupted sleep—and how do you know if it's important unless you check?

Interrupted sleep isn't good for anyone but it's particularly detrimental for children. It disrupts normal sleep cycles that deprive their developing brains of the benefits of deep sleep. It's only during deep sleep, also called "delta sleep" after the high-amplitude, low-frequency brain waves that occur during this phase, that important physiological processes occur. Human growth hormone, which is essential for children, is released during delta sleep. Due to the pulsing manner in which this release takes place, interruption of delta sleep abruptly stops the supply of this requisite hormone.[15]

A 2013 survey of high school students revealed that most respondents got slightly more than six hours of sleep on a school night. (The Centers for Disease Control and Prevention recommends that teens get at least nine hours of sleep per night.[16]) Four out of five reported that they rarely or never get a good night's sleep during the school week. More than half said they were awakened by a text message, phone call, or e-mail on their smartphones because they sleep with them next to their beds.[17]

The survey also asked the students about their presleep activities. The not-shocking results indicated that most were in front of a screen—on the Internet, doing homework on their computer, texting, or social networking. Research indicates that bright screens can disrupt the body's normal release of melatonin, the key hormone that tells your body that it's night, helping to make you sleepy. One study showed that two hours at night in front of an iPad screen at maximum brightness was enough to suppress the normal nighttime release of melatonin.[18] Video games may also be a culprit. Prolonged playing of action video games is known to cause clinically significant sleep disturbances in adolescents.[19]

Buy your teen the alarm clock of her choice so she doesn't have to use her smartphone as an alarm. Discuss the science of sound sleep with her. She may be interested to learn that the growth hormone released during uninterrupted sleep also improves her appearance by helping to tone her muscles.

In the next chapter, we'll talk more about good sleep habits for your entire family, starting with your own. It may be time to buy yourself an alarm clock, too.

Make Yourself See Both Sides

Because of the rapid development of technology, when it comes to issues such as social media and video games, it can feel like you and your teen are more than just a generation apart. You see the reasons for your teen to spend less time posting or gaming online and she sees reasons to spend more time at it. When you comment on her screen-time habits, she defends herself and then you, in turn, argue for your position. In the blink of a screen, you're fighting, or at the very least, you've taken an us-versus-them posture.

When we discussed active listening in Step Three (chapter 6), I described the practice of paraphrasing what your child just said to you so she feels listened to. An active listening technique is a versatile tool during your child's teenage years. Your teen is quite correct that social media and video game playing have benefits and she'll be more inclined to listen to your views if she feels validated by you for hers.

If your teen argues with you in favor of social media and video games, let her know that you agree with her *before* you start to talk about the downside. Don't use the argumentative, "Yes, *but* ______," which immediately undoes the spirit of sharing common ground. Instead, say, "Yes, *and* ______," expressing respect for both sides of the issue.

Choose your times to talk wisely. Late at night, both of you are tired. At the right time and place, in a calm and reasonable conversation, most teens can appreciate the wisdom of a balanced approach.

Work With, Not Against, Your Teen

As your adolescent matures into young adulthood, she needs freedom and autonomy with her online activities so she can explore new possibilities of communciating with social media. Parents face a tough challenge with this, as they recognize the teen brain is built to push the envelope. The temptation is to become more restrictive, supervise more closely, and act more protectively. In some cases, when a teen has demonstrated bad judgment, such as frequenting highly inappropriate sites or putting herself in harm's way, strong measures are in order. But for most teens, overly strict measures lead to a loss of trust, the very opposite of what you want as they venture out on their own.

Understandably, parents are concerned about porngraphy, hook-up sites, and anonymous sites such as Ask.fm and open proxies—that is, a forwarding proxy server that preserves anonymity. (While sites like these are important issues for parents, this book is about attention and discusses only the use of popular recreational sites that most kids use.) Eventually, one way or another, kids will come upon questionable sites and when they do, it's important that they feel safe coming to you.

According to psychologist Catherine Steiner-Adair in *The Big Disconnect*, there are three reasons teens won't go to a parent when they're troubled by an online experience: if they expect the parent to be scary, crazy, or clueless.[20] If you want to be a "go-to parent," your child needs to believe that you won't overreact, be unpredictable, or be dismissive of what she says.

In the right spirit, visiting a social media or gaming site that your teen enjoys can be a bonding experience. Talking about it can build trust. Working together, your efforts are better placed at outsmarting attention snatchers, not each other.

Encourage Your Teen to Ask Metacognitive Questions

Teens are developing the capacity to ask the "What am I *not* doing now?" question, but they're beginners at self-observation, especially when it comes to the magnetic pull of social media and video gaming. You'll still have to step in. One mom was telling me that on a recent school holiday, her son had an online meetup scheduled in a virtual world at 1 P.M. She passed by his room at 10 A.M., and when she saw him at his computer, she knew he'd just stay online until the meetup. She suggested they go shopping for some clothes that he needed and he agreed. Once they were on their way, she was able to talk with him about how, in the future, he could plan ahead on his own to be productive on a morning like that. Her strategy of getting him away from his screen before bringing up the topic paid off.

Although teens are getting better at shifting perspectives and seeing both sides of a story, they'll still be stubbornly one-sided about the sites and games they're hooked on. They'll find support from media reports with headlines like, "Your mother was wrong. Video games aren't bad for you. They're actually making your life better."[21] One young man heard that video games would help him become a surgeon. He used it as a reason to spend more time playing *World of Warcraft*, a case of how a little knowledge can be a dangerous thing.

Research does link playing specific video games with specific surgical skills. A Beth Israel Medical Center study showed that surgical residents and attending physicians with higher scores and more experience playing *MonkeyBall* also completed laparoscopic surgeries faster and made fewer errors.[22] Likewise, a study at the University of Rome showed that after four weeks, surgical residents who practiced Wii games of eye-hand coordination, movement precision, and 3-D visualization and depth perception improved their scores in a laparoscopic surgery simulator.[23] These findings make sense, as laparoscopic surgery employs these skills. However, the subjects of these studies were physicians who had already surmounted the tough hurdles to gain admission and graduate from medical school and qualify for a surgical residency.

In 2013, the average GPA of a college graduate who was admitted to medical school was 3.69, with an average of 3.63 in science classes such as organic chemistry.[24] Students' scores on the MCAT count more than their scores on *MonkeyBall* and for that they need strong voluntary attention.

With so much access to information and learning, our children surprise us with what they know at such young ages. It's easy to forget that they're children and their brains are still under construction. In

The Hurried Child, psychologist David Elkind reminds us, "Children need time to grow, to learn, and to develop. To treat them differently from adults is not to discriminate against them but rather to recognize their special estate."[25]

In the next chapter, we'll look at how you can guide your family to reinforce habits of good attention at home.

9

Step Six
Become a Focus-Friendly Family

The family is one of nature's masterpieces.
—George Santayana

We learn our first definitions of normal behavior from our family. If your family keeps a healthy sleep schedule, eats nutritous food, exercises, reads, and talks intelligently with one another, your children will grow up experiencing these behaviors as normal. If you keep erratic sleep-wake cycles, eat junk food, are sedentary, or interact with screens and not each other, those behaviors will feel normal to your children.

MAKE SLEEP A PRIORITY

In the last chapter, we discussed the problem of disrupted sleep for teens, but poor sleep at night robs every member of your family of the ability to pay attention the next day. Think of the haze you're in at work when you're sleep deprived. Now imagine your child in her classroom in a similar fog, either quietly fading off or acting up to stay alert.

MINIMUM SLEEP REQUIREMENTS NATIONAL GUIDELINES[1]	
Age	**Sleep per Night**
Preschoolers	11 to 12 hours
School-aged	at least 10 hours
Teens	9 to 10 hours
Adults	7 to 8 hours

Children today get an average of one hour less sleep per night than they did thirty years ago.[2] How much of a difference can an hour's worth of sleep make for a grade-schooler? To answer that question, pediatric sleep researcher Avi Sedah had fourth- and sixth-grade students sleep normally for two nights, then sleep for one hour less for three nights. He used an activity monitor to ensure the accuracy of the sleep measures, and he gave students tests of attention the day after their nights of normal sleep and again after their nights of one hour less sleep. The tests showed that a loss of one hour of sleep was equivalent to the loss of two years of maturation on the tests. In other words, sixth-graders performed as if they had the attention of fourth-graders.[3]

What kind of difference can less than a half hour of sleep make to teens? In a survey of over three thousand high school students, those with Cs, Ds, and Fs had an average of twenty-five minutes less sleep than students with As and Bs.[4]

A number of studies link symptoms of inattention with inadequate amounts of sleep.[5] Lack of sleep significantly correlates with severity of symptoms in children with ADHD.[6] Sleep loss and attention disorders have been shown to impact similar brain pathways.[7]

Establish bedtimes for your children and create conditions that support them, such as quiet hours at night in your home. Have a before-bedtime ritual for each child that includes specific tasks such as turning off electronics, personal hygiene routines, reading in bed, hugs, tucking your child in with a goodnight kiss, lullabies for young children, and kind, peaceful words for older children. Avoid bringing up anything new, stimulating, or worrisome at bedtime. Keep your conversations on a positive note.

If your child is resistant to going to bed at night, try different calming approaches such as a short foot massage or an aromatherapy pillow mist. Stay calm yourself. Take into account that no one on the planet is as genius as a child at putting off bedtime. Help your child feel a sense of control by allowing her some choice in her before-bedtime ritual. Allow her to earn reasonable flexibility on weekend bedtimes (that won't shift her sleep-wake cycle) when she cooperates fully on weekday nights.

Some children find it much harder than others to settle down and get to sleep. An analysis of sixteen studies shows that children with attention disorders take longer to fall asleep and show greater resistance to both bedtime and morning awakening.[8] If your child is resistant to waking up in the morning, make sure everything is ready the night before. Take time to work with her on setting her own alarm and having a morning routine. Star charts can help structure morning tasks for young children. Checklists can help for grade-schoolers.

We often think about sleep as the elastic part of the twenty-four-hour cycle. If something needs to be done, we reduce the amount of time we sleep, neglecting the fact we also reduce our clarity and ability for voluntary attention the next day. Our children then adopt our sleep priorities and patterns.

- Keep a reasonable daytime schedule for your family so kids don't have to stay up late to complete homework. Factor in realistic amounts of time for dawdling.
- Plan enough daytime physical activity for your child so that she'll be tired at bedtime.

- Limit your child's caffeine and sugar intake, especially after noon.
- Make your child's room, especially her bed and nightstand, an inviting place to go to sleep.
- Use comforting bedtime rituals as cues for sleep.

Consider adopting this simple nighttime practice: when you tuck your child in at night, together, think of three things you feel grateful for from that day. Researchers have shown that thoughts of gratitude can decrease the amount of time it takes to get to sleep.[9] Plus, it feels good.

SET CLEAR RULES AND LIMITS

In addition to having a set bedtime, children need clear, consistent, age-appropriate rules about completing homework assignments, study time, respectful behavior, healthy eating, physical exercise, and use of digital media. As much as possible, involve your children in making these rules and in reviewing and updating them as your children mature.

Give rules a positive spin. "Your brain can do things that the biggest computers in the world can't do and doing schoolwork is how you make your brain powerful." "I've noticed you don't need to be reminded anymore about sugary snacks. Your beautiful, healthy body says thank you!" "I love you too much to let you turn into a couch potato watching TV."

Choose names for the limits you set about screentime, then be specific about what those rules mean. For example, "quiet hours" might mean no electronics except homework-related Internet from 4 to 6 P.M. for grade-schoolers or no Internet after 11 P.M. for young adults. A "tech holiday" might mean a camping trip with no electronics whatsoever or it could be a day at home with a break from a specific attention snatcher such as video games or TV. A "light tech day" could mean smartphones but no TV or tablets, or it could mean only essential electronic communications. It's best to jot down the rules so that everyone understands.

The American Academy of Pediatrics recommends implementing a "family media-use plan" that's written down and agreed upon by all family members. At their website HealthyChildren.org, they provide tips on how to make one. Their recommendations include keeping screens out of kids' bedrooms, coviewing media with kids, and having a media curfew. Letting kids know what doctors recommend might help them accept unpopular rules.

Rules are beneficial because when you make them, you're in a rational state of mind—clear about the goals that are most important for your family and what it takes to achieve them. Later, in the presence of a hot stimulus, you and your family have the rule to connect you back to those goals and away from temptations like attention snatchers.

Some families find that it's helpful to have regularly scheduled times to meet and discuss decisions such as house rules, schedules, and vacation plans. In my practice, I've seen parents who were initally skeptical that the idea could work, but they tried having a weekly or biweekly family meeting and were pleasantly surprised at the results. A good day to do this is on a Sunday so you can preview the week ahead. You can organize and post schedules and rules that last until the next family meeting.

It's best to keep family meetings short and focused on the tasks at hand. Give each family member a chance to bring up reasonable concerns about matters like fairness and flexibility. Kids sometimes offer creative solutions. Not long ago, one parent told me that her family was discussing the use of cell phones at the dinner table. They had a rule against it, but it seemed that lately everyone had a special reason for taking an important call or returning a text that couldn't wait. The mom told them about an article she'd read. Silicon Valley executives were trying to break the habit of using their smartphones at lunches, so they made a rule that whoever answered a call or text had to pick up the check. The kids suggested that they adapt the idea to meals in their home. Whoever needed to make an exception and use their smartphone would have to clean up after dinner.

ENJOY FAMILY MEALS TOGETHER

For many families, it's no longer practical for everyone to eat dinner at the same time every night. Parents work late or have long commutes. Kids have complicated schedules filled with extracurricular activities. But every family can have dinner together on some nights, and there are solid reasons for you to make this happen. Family meals provide your child with a sense of security and stability, family unity and identity.[10]

As we spend more time interacting with screens, we spend less time interacting in person, especially with the members of our own family. At family meals, we stay in touch with each other's day-to-day lives and feelings, and by doing so, we share important knowledge about what it's like to be human—the kind of information you can't get from Google. We transmit values and attitudes from one generation to the next at the family table.

The family meal is a rare opportunity for children to practice patience, respect, and listening skills in conversation with others. These habits will endure because they're being formed consistently over time. Kids are strengthening their voluntary attention. Conversing with adults, they cultivate critical thinking, reflection, and the ability to articulate their own ideas in an atmosphere of emotional safety.

If scheduling meals together is a challenge for you and your family, make it your goal to have at least three family meals per week. Keep it simple, so you can reach that goal. No one is counting the number of healthy take-out meals you serve.

Whether you're among the lucky families who can eat together every night or those who can do it less often, guard the quality of your family mealtime. Use this valuable opportunity to create comfort and closeness with your children.

- Don't squander this precious time with TV, texting, or any other electronic distraction.
- Don't be critical, argue, or put your children on the spot.
- Don't allow your own tensions to come with you to the table.

- Do practice eye contact, careful listening, and sustained attention.
- Do ask nonthreatening questions that spark cheerful conversation.
- Do create a warm and relaxing atmosphere.

Provide lots of positive comments, even statements as simple as how nice it feels when everyone is at the table. Give kids as much say as possible in decisions such as the time, menu, and appropriate background music. Light a candle on the table to signal that it's time to stash the smartphones and start sharing a meal together.

How can you promote intelligent, imaginative, and positive conversation?

- Use old family recipes to start conversations about relations and family stories.
- Use ethnic recipes to start conversations about cultural traditions.
- Talk about upbeat stories in the news, such as a space launch or an eclipse.
- Talk about upcoming birthdays, holidays, and vacations.
- Ask everyone, "What was the best part of your day?"

If one family member isn't talking much, address him by name and ask an interesting, age-appropriate question.

- For very young children, ask "If" questions, such as, "If you could have any superpower, what would it be?" or "If you could be an animal for a day, what would you be?"
- For older children, ask questions about their individual interests, such as sports, music, books they're reading, their favorite video games, or upcoming parties and events.

No matter how weary you are from the day, set an example of listening attentively at the table. Your children will learn to do the same for you.

MULTIGENERATIONAL VIDEO GAMING: GIVE IT YOUR BEST SHOT

Nine-year-old Nick missed his dad, who was deployed overseas. His mom was concerned about the growing number of hours he spent playing video games. She understood it was Nick's way of feeling connected to his father. Even though it was seldom possible for them to play together due to time-zone differences and scheduling conflicts, Nick and his dad chatted about gaming. It was a bond they shared. At the same time, Nick's mom was worried that Nick was isolating himself from others by gaming. She herself felt distant from her son, who was in the next room.

Nick's parents talked about his gaming, and his dad suggested that his mom start to game with their son, too. At first, Nick's mom objected. It seemed to her this would make the problem worse, not better. But she went along with the idea and was really glad she did. Nick was happy to teach her, and she discovered that gaming was beneficial for her son in several unexpected ways.

First, it was more fun than she thought it would be and both of them needed more fun. What struck her the most, though, was a shift in the way that Nick experienced himself when he played. Nick was prone to feeling sorry for himself at times: "Why me? Why does my dad have to be away?" Gaming put him in an active role and cultivated a sense of himself as a champion, facing challenges and conquering new levels of play. This, in turn, helped to shift his mind-set from victim to hero.

Nick's mom used this insight to talk with Nick, to understand his feelings better. She helped her son connect with feeling proud of his dad, which, in turn, helped Nick approach kids and make new friends.

When I bring up the topic of multigenerational gaming, parents usually fall into two camps—those who already play with their kids and can't wait to tell me about it, and those who back away saying, "It's not my thing," or like Nick's mom, "I'm trying to get him to play less, not more!" Or they express resignation, "He'd never want to play with me!"

"It's not my thing." If you asked your child to try something new and

he replied, "It's not my thing," would you wonder what's really going on? Would you check with him to see if he's afraid he won't be good at it? If you anticipate that the rules will be too complicated or it'll be too hard for you to keep up, that makes gaming an even better parent-child activity. Your child gets to teach you. That's money in the bank for all those occasions when you need to teach your child. Are you afraid of feeling embarrassed? Again, it doesn't get better than laughing at ourselves as we play together with our children. Don't get stuck on the word "video." Tune in to the words "game" and "play" and have a good time.

"*I'm trying to get him to play less, not more.*" Is your true goal to get your child to play less by directly supervising his behavior, or for him to make good choices on his own when you're not there? In Step Three (chapter 6), we discussed the difference between performance and learning. If all you do is set strict rules about gaming, your child will perform by complying in enforceable circumstances. However, if you game with your child, discuss gaming together, deconstruct its elements, strengthen his ability to break the trance and think critically about video games, and share common ground so you respect each other's points of view, you're helping him learn to play responsibly on his own.

"*He'd never want to play with me!*" On the contrary, according to the results of a National Science Foundation study, multigenerational gameplay is more often initiated by children than parents.[11] This finding isn't all that surprising, is it? Think like your child. You enjoy playing. You like to have your parents' attention. And if you can get your parents hooked, you can take them and their wallets with you when you go to GameStop.

Researchers at Arizona State University use focus groups to study the ways that generations interact when playing off-the-shelf video games—for instance, how parents and kids talk about their decisions and what strategies to take next. They maintain that the same video games that parents say are separating them from their kids can actually bring them closer together.[12]

Another study at Brigham Young University showed positive effects for parents coplaying with their teenage girls.[13] Researchers from several major universities have entered joint ventures to study the benefits of multigenerational play for parents, grandparents, and kids.[14]

When you game with your kids, you share experiences in the virtual world that can help your children in the real world, but they're too young to make those leaps on their own. For example, when your child is discouraged or frustrated by a bad grade, a rejection, or an error, you can remind him that the way he's gotten better in his favorite video game is by losing over and over again. You can say these words if you don't game with him, but they'll just be words. If you game together, your words communicate a shared truth and are more likely to reach him.

Jordan Shapiro, a tech blogger for *Forbes*, games with his sons, ages six and eight years old, and describes how he uses the framework of the game world to help his sons solve problems in the real one:

> I might ask my son to draw pictures of a video game in which the goal is to solve a playground dispute. This serves two functions. First, this kind of imaginative exercise provides my son with some objective distance from his life-world problems. Second, it allows my son to reimagine his everyday situations in a way that is empowering; in a video game, his actions impact the game's outcome.[15]

If you don't game with your children, you're missing many teachable moments and some of your best opportunities to help them develop metacognition, the ability to think about their thinking. When you and your child talk about the elements of a game, especially what makes it hard to resist, you're fostering their awareness. Having been in the trance together, when you emerge from the trance, you can take a step back together and self-observe.

As we discussed in Step Five (chapter 8), if you're not a gamer, you can start with an easy genre, such as a game in which you're physically active or a game with simple rules like a race. If you gamed as a kid, you'll be amazed at new versions of old favorites such as *SimCity*. Most kids who like virtual worlds join the ones that their friends like to frequent. Ask your child to show you around his favorite virtual world and get ready to be astonished by what he can build and do there. Don't jump into deconstructing a game until you get to know it, see its merits, and appreciate what it means to your child.

Talk with your kids about what it takes to construct a video game. Ask them what kind of game they would create. Explore books about game design with them. Many are available in plain language—no programming knowledge required. In the process of imagining new video games, kids deconstruct the ones they already play. The more they identify what hooks a player into a game, the more they build an observer-self for gaming. We'll talk more about this in the next chapter.

You'll still need to ask the question, "What are we *not* doing now?" for your child. You, not your child, know the value of board games, card games, blocks, art materials, and other activities that build patience and perseverance without the aid of electronic stimulation and attention-grabbing cues. You understand what games of pretend, hide-and-seek, tag, and other excuses to run around the backyard give your child that complement the skills he's learning on his gaming console.

When playing games with your child, keep the right mind-set, as we discussed in Step One (chapter 4). As Frank Lloyd Wright once observed, "The trick is to grow up without getting old."

CHOOSE OUTDOOR HOLIDAYS AND VACATIONS

In Step Three (chapter 6), we discussed a model digital classroom that I visited here in San Diego. I was impressed to learn that their class trip was a camping adventure to a nearby island known for its natural beauty and conservancy-protected wildlife. By being tech-free in the great outdoors, these children have the invaluable opportunity to be unplugged in the world of nature, and contrast it with what it's like when they're plugged in.

Give your children this same opportunity. Take them out into nature for a vacation. Go on a camping trip or to a lodge at a national, state, or county park away from the ubiquitous screens in cities and suburbs. If you choose a sleepover summer camp for your child, find one that doesn't permit electronics. Some camps have created a solution that allows parents and kids speedy communication but keeps the experience tech-free. A parent can e-mail, but the e-mail is printed and given to the child; the child can write out a message that a counselor then e-mails to the parent.

When you and your children are outside together, feel the replenishment of attention that time in nature gives us. Researchers of attention restoration theory (ART) are looking into how this occurs.

To test ART, psychologists at the University of Michigan designed an experiment that began with giving subjects mental tasks until their attention was fatigued. Then, one group of subjects walked through the Ann Arbor Arboretum park for an hour, while the other group walked through downtown Ann Arbor for the same amount of time. When they returned, the subjects who walked through the park had significantly higher scores on standardized tests of voluntary attention than the downtown city walkers, thus demonstrating greater attention restoration.[16]

Scientists who study ART call the intriguing, soothing stimuli of nature "soft fascinations." According to ART, outside in nature, soft fascinations *gently* grab our involuntary attention. This is in contrast to the way that excitatory stimuli, such as the electronically generated sights and sounds from a screen, *dramatically* grab it. As long as these soft fascinations—the pleasing sights and sounds of trees, clouds, birds, breezes, babbling brooks, and waves of the ocean—hold our involuntary attention peacefully, we have no need to exert voluntary attention unless we so desire. In this way, brain pathways for voluntary attention get a needed rest, depleted brain chemicals replenish, and our capacity for voluntary attention is restored. A systematic study of ART is being conducted at the University of Exeter Medical School in the United Kingdom.[17]

Time in nature is a brain tune-up for every member of your family, but it's especially crucial for children, whose brains are still developing. When you and your family have a choice, choose nature. In the words of Ralph Waldo Emerson, "In the woods we return to reason and faith."

As your children get older, you'll need to update your practices as a focus-friendly family to respect their growing independence. You'll also need to adapt to the not-yet-invented next big innovation about to enter your home. In chapter 10, we'll discuss how you can stay positive yet prepared for the rapid changes yet to come.

10

Step Seven
Celebrate Success but Prepare for Stronger Snatchers

The future belongs to those who believe in the beauty of their dreams.
—Eleanor Roosevelt

Sometimes, the reason we escape into TV screens and Facebook newsfeeds is to get away from feeling like we can't do all there is to get done, or that we're not good enough. We each have an inner critic for just about every aspect of our lives, but when it comes to parenting, that nagging voice can be merciless.

Your child starts to text in front of company and your inner critic tells you that you haven't raised her with manners. Her teacher e-mails you that she's distracted at school and your inner critic tells you it's your fault.

This chapter asks you to call on two other inner voices that deserve to be heard: your inner backer and your inner coach. Your inner backer wants you to pay attention to the things you're doing right. And your inner coach wants you to keep doing them, as you face the unknown future.

GIVE YOURSELF ENCOURAGEMENT AND A PAT ON THE BACK

In the world of adults, when the going gets tough, some kind soul somewhere will offer a sympathetic remark. When you've done an outstanding job, eventually someone will notice and acknowledge your efforts. But when it's just you and your child, you're unlikely to hear words like, "You had a complicated scheduling conflict today and managed the near-impossible task of taking care of my time demands, as well as those of my sibling, without plopping either of us down in front of the TV." No, if anyone is going to notice and appreciate your feat, it's got to be you.

Asking you to give yourself credit is not just a bunch of fluff. Attention is a powerful reinforcer. Behaviors, *including your own*, to which you give the most attention, are the ones you're most likely to repeat. If you let your inner critic have its way and you squander all your attention on what you didn't get done this afternoon and how you had to use a screen as a babysitter again, you strengthen your inclination to repeat that behavior. Instead, if you listen to your inner coach, you'll give most of your attention to the things you *did* accomplish, appreciate the success you had, and be more inclined to keep on succeeding.

In my practice, I ask parents to actively shift their focus from the hard work of parenting to their reasons for doing it. At times, it can make a real difference. Positive self-talk can help. See the box on the next page for a few examples to get you started.

Usually, you and your child's other parent know your child better than anyone else. You're positioned like no one else to appreciate what it takes to raise your unique child. You know the specific ways your child will try your patience and push your buttons. A compliment from one parent to another means a lot, because you're getting that compliment from someone who understands the challenge. Whether or not you see eye-to-eye on anything else, parent-to-parent, pat each other on the back. If your child's other parent is absent, double your efforts to value yourself as a parent.

Positive Self-Talk for Parents

Even when I'm angry, I'm grateful for my children.
Caring for children is exhausting, but small potatoes compared to sharing in their wonder.
Yes, it's frustrating. Yes, it's hard work. And yes, I'm the one who gets to see them learn and grow.
I appreciate everything I've done today to be a good parent, and if my kids knew what I know, they'd appreciate me too.
I'm thankful to be a parent. The responsibilities are great but the rewards are greater.

APPRECIATE YOUR CHILD'S EFFORTS

Your thirteen-year-old daughter used to watch TV every night, but lately, she's been reading in the evenings instead. You want to express appreciation for her efforts, so you say:

a. Thank you for not watching so much TV every night.
b. Thank you for starting to read more books.
c. I think the way you've stopped watching TV every night is terrific.
d. Can't help but notice you've been reading more lately. That book is part of a series, isn't it? What's it about?
e. All of the above

A thirteen-year-old girl is well past the age of reason. As we discussed in Step Five (chapter 8), language that implies that you, not she, is responsible for her habits, is now counterproductive. So (a) and (b) might be good answers for your preschooler but not your teen. Choice (c) is on the cusp. If you and your daughter have established common ground about reducing TV watching and both of you are making this effort together, it's OK as an answer. It's probably a better response for a grade-schooler, though, than a teen. Through her eyes, it sets you up as the judge, so instead of feeling appreciated, she might silently be saying to herself, "Who asked you?"

Teens will be more open to a response that's descriptive, not evaluative, like answer (d). By asking about the book she's reading, your underlying message is, "You're acting like an adult and I'm treating you like one." Your undivided attention is rewarding and the expression of your interest in her reading tells her that you appreciate the choice she's making.

- Don't praise children for being smart or for any other trait over which they have no control.
- Don't give gratuitous praise.
- Don't let too many corrections go by without saying something positive about your child's behavior, especially at homework time.
- Do notice and acknowledge your child's efforts, especially in the face of frustration and failure.
- Do be specific and age-appropriate when you express recognition of your child's good choices and hard work.
- Do stay aware of the ratio between critical comments and complimentary ones, especially in times of stress.

TURN BAD CHOICES INTO GOOD CHOICES

Zoe, age five, enjoyed watching cartoons on the DVD player in the back seat of her family's new car, and her parents liked the break it gave them to be on their own in the front. Soon, however, Zoe wouldn't ride in the car without it being on. Her parents decided to limit her use of the screen to long trips or exceptional circumstances. They offered alternatives—listening to music, audiobooks, and playing guessing games together—but Zoe got demonstrably upset, crying for cartoons when she got bored in the car. Zoe's mom did her best to stay calm and teach her daughter to calm down, too, but Zoe could not be dissuaded.

Zoe's mom realized that they were falling into a negative habit of Zoe getting too much attention for her bad behavior. She was running out of patience, which fueled Zoe to subconsciously push her buttons even more. She needed to break this pattern—to shift from giving her attention to Zoe's wrong choices and onto Zoe's efforts to make better ones. She had a plan, but first she had to block out time with Zoe *before* they got into the car.

She asked her daughter, "When you get tired of being in the car and you want to watch cartoons but you know that's not allowed, it's a bad choice to start screaming and crying. What does a good choice look like?"

"Play songs," Zoe answered.

"Yes, that's right. And what if you feel like screaming or crying?" Zoe's mom continued. "A bad choice is to give in and yell about wanting cartoons. What does a good choice look like?"

She helped her daughter think of words like "quiet," "be a big girl," "think about the words to the songs," "sing along," and "smile." They drew a picture together of Zoe singing in the car with a smile and labeled it "Good Choice."

Later, in the car, when Zoe started to act cranky, Zoe's mom asked her, "What does a good choice look like?" Having laid the groundwork for this moment, Zoe's mom could now keep her attention on rewarding even the smallest effort Zoe made to recall the picture. If necessary, she could hand her daughter the picture and ask her to describe it. Everyone's attention would be on the good choice, not the bad one.

You can use the technique of "bad choice, good choice" in any circumstance in which you find yourself rewarding your child's bad behavior with your attention. It works for older children, too. Have them write out their description of a good choice, draw a cartoon, sing lyrics from a song, or use any other method to illustrate what a good choice looks like in a particular situation. The time it takes for you to coach your child to describe or draw what a good choice looks like is a solid investment that yields high returns in the future.

One mother in my practice adapted a flash-card version of the technique. When her son made a bad choice, he drew a picture of it with a big X through it on one side of an index card. On the other side, he drew a picture of the good choice. After a while he had a small stack. When he was about to make a bad choice, he and his mom gave each other a knowing look, and his mom nodded toward the deck. It's best to keep a calm, positive tone when using "bad choice, good choice." Think of it as if you were correcting your child's tennis stroke or piano technique—an exercise in skill-building.

GIVE YOUR CHILD MENTAL TOOLS

Enrich Your Child's Attention Vocabulary. Help young children become more aware of their own attention. Use words like "focused" or "distracted," "on-task" or "off-task," and "undivided attention" or "divided attention." Preface these terms with "*choose* to be" to increase their awareness that they're in charge of these attentional states. When your child is old enough to understand the concept, explain the difference to him between "voluntary attention" and "involuntary attention."

Help your older child understand what it's like to be "understimulated" or "overstimulated." In Step Five (chapter 8), we discussed the upside-down U-curve that describes your child's focus zone of just-right stimulation. The fact that world-class athletes use this framework gives it a positive context for kids. It could come in handy if your child insists he can concentrate on his homework just as well if he's also watching TV. You might use it to discuss with him how music with lyrics is more distracting than music without them, and why multitasking takes a toll on accuracy.

Establish the Difference between Avoidance and Taking a Break. In my practice, I have to talk with kids about things they've done—topics they'd rather avoid, like inappropriate behavior, a failing grade, or being suspended from school. Before I can apply a technique like "bad choice, good choice," I have to understand, from their perspective, how the bad choice happened. I need to know the starting place for how much responsibility they're ready to take for it. I create the most pleasant conditions I can, but kids still get embarrassed and try to dodge the subject. To help them see what they're doing and keep things honest between us, I identify their avoidance in a compassionate way. I let them know that what we're doing can be hard at times and assure them we can take breaks to relieve the tension.

Using simple terms, I explain the difference between avoidance and taking a break: You take a break with the clear intention of returning to a task you'd rather avoid. When we break, I state our clear intention: "Let's go for a walk together and pick this up again in about ten minutes." "Let's take a break and play bop-it for five minutes. I'll set the timer on my phone." Being kids, they try to extend these breaks and turn them into avoidance. When we return to the tough topic, they resist. I remind them of the difference between avoidance and a break and keep a steady stream of acknowledgment for their efforts to stick with a difficult subject. I let them know they can suggest taking a break, too.

When I see that a kid really gets the difference, I feel optimistic about the progress we're going to make from then on. It means that he's functioning at a new level of awareness, responsibility, and self-control. When he bears the discomfort of owning up to his mistakes, I say, "That's a gutsy thing to do."

You can use a similar approach with your children at home. One of the most effective mental tools you can give your child is a blame-free, clear, and honest understanding of avoidance.

Everyone puts off tasks that require voluntary attention because voluntary attention requires work. Procrastination is part of the human condition; guilt just compounds it. Let your child know that you feel the pull of avoidance, too. We all do. Then, in a matter-of-fact way, explain the difference between avoidance—which sabotages voluntary attention—and taking a break—which helps to keep it strong.

Teach Your Child How to Reset. I once worked with a junior high science teacher who had received an award as the result of high ratings from both students and parents. She told me about a practice she uses in the classroom called "change-of-state." Junior high science demands strong voluntary attention from kids, which can be hard for them to sustain for an entire class period. When the energy in her class gets too low, she calls for a change-of-state. A student leads the class in a break that can take no more than three minutes. It can be jumping jacks or a skit or telling jokes or playing a song while everyone dances.

Each student is responsible for choosing and leading the change-of-state. The kids take it on like a contest, trying to outdo each other with creative and cool ideas. They know when their turn is coming up, and make the most of their chance to lead the class. I was particularly interested in what one class parent had to say. She reported that in grade school when her son got tired of homework, he wanted to watch TV for a short while. As long as he was keeping up with his assignments, she allowed this. Now, she said, since starting this class, he chooses more active and interesting ways to take his breaks. She's noticed that his attitude, as well as his longevity for doing homework, has improved.

You can create your own version of change-of-state at home. Teach your child to recognize when he's getting drawn to distraction because his energy is low. Then, take turns creating a three-minute energy boost to get him back into his focus zone. Until he's mature enough, keep an eye on his energy level for him. Paradoxically, sometimes when kids are tired, they become hyperactive instead of slowing down. Brain scientists believe this is an attempt by their nervous system to rev themselves up and out of a state of boredom. Either way, it's a signal for a change-of-state. Just like a computer with a frozen screen, a brain that's stuck needs a reboot.

BE PREPARED FOR THE GREAT UNKNOWN

What will the next big thing be? Whatever it is, chances are, it will catch on quicker than a video gone viral on YouTube. When texting was first introduced, teens sent and received about the same number of texts as they did phone calls. Only two years later, teens sent and received an average of 3,146 texts per month (approximately ten texts per waking, nonschool hour) while making and receiving 191 phone calls monthly.[1]

While we don't yet know exactly what new technology lies ahead, what we do know is that technology is power, and there will be a bright side and a shadowy side that we'll need to manage. For example, those in the know predict the next big thing could be virtual reality (VR) games that are accessible and affordable—a dream that's been alive since our first peek at a holodeck aboard the starship *Enterprise*.

In 2014, the Oculus Rift—innovative VR hardware—sold over eighty-five thousand prototypes to developers who were adapting games for its use.[2] It has huge potential as a learning tool. It can simulate dangerous and difficult environments. NASA uses the Oculus Rift to train astronauts to operate rovers and work with robots in outer space.[3] Its applications are as wide-ranging as our own imaginations. For instance, one young illustrator who creates art for video games heard about the Oculus Rift and obtained a headset for her dying grandmother, who had been immobile and housebound since being diagnosed with cancer. She gave her grateful grandmother a VR experience of walking and climbing without pain and visiting a garden and the ocean one last time before she died.[4]

Like any power, we'll need to learn how to keep VR in check. Kids may use it to enrich their experience of the real world—for example, to explore times and places they can't visit in person. Or they may use it to immerse themselves in games. Their biggest challenge is summed up by the headline of a 2014 review of the Oculus Rift in the tech blog *Gizmodo*: "I Wore the New Oculus Rift and I Never Want to Look at Real Life Again."[5]

Kids today are already bored with ordinary life as compared with the high-stim action of video games. When they're able to virtually ride rollercoasters, leap from rooftop to rooftop, or explore outer space, what will keep them from falling down the rabbit hole of virtual reality, except for the self-control skills that they're building today?

DON'T UNDERESTIMATE ATTENTION SNATCHERS

Have you ever watched a movie trailer or a Super Bowl ad that you just couldn't turn away from? Brain scientists have teamed up with corporations to form the fast-growing industry of neuromarketing, whose sole purpose is to break down your resistance. Using brain-imaging techniques, neuromarketers test and tweak commercials by recording the changes that take place in a viewer's brain as he watches. They look for maximum activation in the pleasure centers of the brain and lots of action in the sensory cortex.

Brain scientists bring highly specialized knowledge and skills to neuromarketing, and corporations bring the capital. It costs up to a thousand dollars per hour for researchers to run a functional MRI scan, and studies often use twenty to thirty subjects.[6] Brain-tracking reveals triggers to consumers' desires and purchase decisions that are unknown to the consumers themselves. In other words, neuromarketers are demonstrating that they know more about what we buy than we ourselves do. For example, in one study, adolescents were asked to listen to new tracks by relatively unknown recording artists while being scanned by an MRI. They were also asked which of the songs they liked and disliked. The MRI results showed activation of a specific reward-related region of the brain, the ventral striatum, but it didn't correspond to what the teens said they liked or disliked. The sales of those recordings were tracked for three years. Purchases correlated significantly with the MRI results but not with the songs the teens said they liked. The MRI results predicted purchase decisions not just for the teens in the study but for the population at large.[7]

In his 2013 best seller, *Salt, Sugar, Fat*,[8] investigative reporter Michael Moss explains how large food manufacturers use scientific rigor to arrive at precise formulations of these three ingredients to make processed foods that keep you wanting more. They seek what they call "the bliss point," which evokes a measurable physical and emotional response. Moss says that the food engineers are not villains: they just want to sell more product.

With the help of neuromarketers, designers of media products are identifying our digital bliss points. They, too, just want to increase sales. But it's up to us to respect their specialized expertise, application of advanced brain-imaging technology, and huge financial investments. They keenly compete for our dollars, our involuntary attention and—of greatest concern to parents—our children's involuntary attention.

TEACH YOUR CHILD TO DECONSTRUCT DIGITAL MEDIA

In the *Wizard of Oz,* the moment Toto pulls down the curtain to reveal an ordinary man who stands at the controls of a throne apparatus is iconic. "Pay no attention to that man behind the curtain," he says, ducking away. "The great and powerful Oz has spoken." But Dorothy is persistent. "Who are you?"

When you and your child are engaged in digital media together, look for appropriate opportunites to deconstruct TV ads and shows, video games, headlines of posts online, or any other screen activity designed to hook and reel you in. Enjoy time together in the trance, too, but when the moment is right, help your child pull back the curtain and, like Dorothy, ask questions so she can't be fooled.

From time to time, when you watch TV together, take apart ads for food and toys. When you watch a reality show, discuss what's real and what's staged. Don't shame kids about their naïveté or their choices of programs. You'll drive them to hide what they're doing from you, at a time when they need your guidance the most. In Step Six (chapter 9), we discussed multigenerational gaming and the opportunities it affords to enjoy, appreciate, and also deconstruct games with your kids. The same is true for viewing TV.

Help your child understand that product placement that appears casual is not. When you watch movies or TV together, make a game of finding product placement. Give young children hints at first, if they need them, such as looking for labels on what people eat or drink, or the logo on a car or a computer. Notice how reruns have product placement newly embedded in the background of scenes, such as once-nondescript storefronts that now appear as brand-name stores.

Go online with your child, and when the opportunity presents itself, discuss how most headlines are sensationalized and many posts are emotionally manipulative. Talk about who profits from online ads and how users can unwittingly be used as unpaid salespeople when they repost or click on "share." Ask your child if she thinks product reviews can be bought, and if there are clues to tell the difference between a purchased review and an unbiased one.

Stay informed so you can have knowledgeable conversations with your child. Discuss the economics of digital media—for example, how popular video games make big money and exercise political clout. The global market for video games was approximately $67 billion in 2012, with a five-year growth estimate to $82 billion.[9] In 2013 in the United States, the Entertainment Software Association spent roughly $3.9 million in lobbying efforts.[10]

I noticed in a recent issue of our local city recreation guide that alongside kids' camps for sports, music, and arts and crafts, this year's offerings include video game design. Kids ages ten to seventeen can learn how to produce their own games and publish them as apps for handheld devices. Experiences like these give kids behind-the-scenes lessons that keep them practiced at taking a step back and seeing game design from an empowering perspective. No longer are they just players; they're the creators, too, and must analyze games with the detachment of an objective observor.

Wouldn't it be something if, in addition to demystifying video games, learning to create games earns your child a cut in those lucrative industry profits. The Oculus Rift (the previously mentioned innovative VR hardware) was developed by a twenty-two-year-old who took apart old VR headsets in his parents' garage. In 2014, Facebook bought the Oculus company for $2 billion.[11]

KNOW WHAT YOUR INDIVIDUAL CHILD NEEDS

You can learn a lot about your child when you spend time next to him discovering his digital habits. Get to know what he's really good at and what draws him in. The key to your child sharing screentime with you is your nonjudgmental attitude. If you're there to get to know him, not to criticize him, he won't have to protect and defend his online behavior.

A number of years ago in my practice, I was seeing a thirteen-year-old boy we'll call Joey. He was a bright kid who was underachieving at school. Joey was impulsive. He wasn't a good listener, wouldn't read directions, and didn't take good notes. He consistently overestimated how much he could keep in his head and underestimated how much time he needed to complete assignments.

In fourth grade, Joey had been diagnosed with ADHD, but medication didn't help improve his study habits. When his parents and teachers tried to work with him, Joey accepted their correction but continued to make the same mistakes. It was difficult to have a productive conversation with Joey. He wouldn't stay on topic for very long.

Joey enjoyed spending time in a virtual world called Habbo Hotel. Preteens and teens use it to connect socially. At Habbo, you create your own avatar (your Habbo Hotel character). You also design your own room and move around to different common areas called "official rooms." There, you meet others who are also logged on. As of 2012, Habbo Hotel had 273 million users in 150 countries.[12] (In recent years, it had to take corrective action to keep its content appropriate, but my work with Joey had nothing to do with that.)

After trying all sorts of approaches, I decided to suggest that Joey and I go online and visit this site together. I checked with Joey's parents and they were all for it. I wasn't sure how Joey would respond, but he said OK and we logged on. Joey led his avatar to one of the official rooms, which was full of other avatars having conversations. Users type in what they want their avatar to say, and the words appear in cartoon balloons that quickly float up the page, like high-speed movie credits.

Joey was capable of typing fast to chat with others while at the same time talking with me. As I got used to the format, I noticed that Joey was behaving in a pattern. He had his avatar enter a room, choose a girl avatar, and approach her. Sooner or later, and sometimes immediately, the girl would shake him off and move on. Joey persisted. The girl avatar would ignore Joey, get rude, or disappear.

I then realized Joey was a Habbo Hotel stalker, but not a mean one. He followed these girls with two parts playfulness, two parts pride, and one part impish glee. We returned to Habbo Hotel a number of times. The more I listened, the more Joey talked about his experiences there. I gently asked him about following the girls. He confidently told me, "They like that." He was convinced this was the way to play the game.

I continued to ask nonthreatening questions, encouraging Joey to be open to seeing his actions from different points of view. I asked him what he thought about how the other guy avatars approached girls and he shrugged me off. It dawned on me that although Joey said he was reading the fast-moving words in the balloons, he was scanning and not actually registering what was being said. He didn't have much patience for listening in the real world. Why would it be different in this virtual world? With so many avatars speaking, the dialogue moved up the screen rapidly. A user who was trying could barely keep up, and Joey didn't appear to be trying all that much.

In the past, Joey had good-naturedly agreed with me that at school he was better at "transmit" than "receive." I brought this up, and he agreed that this was true in his virtual world as well. We decided to spend some time "lurking" at Habbo—that is, observing without participating. We started to select and read the words of other avatars in the balloons as they flew up and off the screen. Joey continued to refrain from typing so we could talk about the snippets of conversation we read together.

We kidded around about some of them, but also looked at how other avatars approached each other in the official rooms. I asked Joey what he would do if a girl stayed around so they could get to know each other better. Joey said he didn't know—which could have been part of the reason he was sabotaging his own efforts.

We continued to lurk and talk, and Joey told me he tried new approaches at home during the week. He was beginning to wait before typing the words he thought up to say. He told me that sometimes he just said what he heard someone else say in another room to start a conversation. "It's lame, but I do it anyway 'cause it works."

Joey and I talked about using some of his new ideas about waiting, observing, and trying out what others did in real life, too. Joey was still making impulsive errors in judgment at school but he started to take it down a notch. He'll always be spontaneous and want to do things his own way, but, at Habbo, Joey seemed to realize that you can learn from others. He also experienced the value of looking before you leap.

BE PREPARED BUT NOT PUSHY

The Khan Academy is a free, nonprofit website with thousands of short video tutorials from easy to advanced levels on a wide range of subjects. It began when Salman Khan, a former hedge-fund analyst with degrees in engineering and computer science, was asked by his cousin in another state to help her with math. He made video clips of clear, accurate, friendly lessons and sent them to her. Soon, other relatives and friends asked, too. He began to make short instructive videos that students could access at any time, pause as needed, and play and replay to view whatever parts they wanted. Today, Khan Academy YouTube videos have more than 400 million views, with approximately 2 million subscribers.[13]

Some teachers use Khan Academy lessons to "flip" their classrooms. In other words, instead of using class time to deliver instruction, they assign a video tutorial as homework and the next day they cover the practice problems in class. That way, they can give their attention to students as they apply the lesson. Last year, flipped classrooms received coverage from the national news outlets and many parents were introduced to the Khan Academy for the first time. Some enthused parents tried to get their kids to watch the videos for enrichment, but they didn't have much luck. That's because kids use resources like Khan on an as-needed basis. When your child is stuck trying to solve a quadratic equation, that's the time to give him the link to a trig lesson on that specific type of problem. He'll see the value of that lesson because it meets his need. *Then* he'll incorporate Khan tutorials as he needs them in the future.

The same is true of other high-quality websites, such as MOOCs (massive open online courses) and also productivity software. You can learn more about these by googling them and talking with other parents. Do the footwork so that you've got some good choices handy when the opportunity presents itself. Then, *carpe diem*. When your child is amenable because he's in need, you've got tools to put in his hands.

One mom told me that her teenage daughter enjoyed Facebook but was becoming aware that she was using it to procrastinate when she hit the hardest parts of her homework assignments. Her mom had heard about browser extensions that limit time on recreational sites and tried to find one that her daughter might like. She found a free Chrome extension called "Kill News Feed" and suggested it to her daughter. It would still allow her the Facebook functions she might want to use intentionally, but it would replace the continuous stream of posts from her friends with the message: "Don't get distracted by Facebook."

They went online together to see if it was easy to turn the extension on and off. (It is.) On the page with the download, her daughter read positive reviews by other users who said they'd been procrastinating with Facebook newsfeeds, too. Reading them, she felt validated for what she was doing. Also, the reviews helped her to regard the extension as a friendly and useful tool.

KNOW WHAT COMPUTER SKILLS YOUR CHILD IS LEARNING AT SCHOOL

Does your child's school offer classes in coding? Teaching computer programming to students from kindergarten through twelfth grade has become a global educational movement. Computer science is now a part of England's primary school curriculum. A number of other nations include it in their high school syllabi—for example, Israel, Germany, Denmark, Australia, and New Zealand.[14]

Here in the United States, school districts in major cities, such as New York and Chicago, offer high school coding classes. Educational policies are changing so that credits for computer science are no longer regarded as electives but counted the same as math and science.[15]

The movement is not without controversy. Advocates point out that coding is a life skill in the world in which our children are growing up. If they enter the tech sector, they've got a solid foundation. If they don't, they still benefit because coding teaches logic. Opponents say that the classes employ teaching software made up of games that don't teach actual skills. Also, they're wary of corporate involvement in deciding what kids learn in school and how they learn it.

Stay informed about computer science at your child's school. You can learn more at Code.org, a nonprofit site for educators and parents that's funded by major tech companies. One benefit of coding is that it helps a student change perspectives and shift roles from consumer to creator of software.

As more teachers become trained in educational technology, we'll see more applications of technology in classrooms. Many schools now have interactive whiteboards, which show anything that's on a computer screen and allows teachers and students to draw, write, and manipulate images on the board. These interactive boards—often called "smart boards," after the popular brand name—can have accessories such as a document camera, student response systems, and software for students to compile virtual multimedia notebooks.

Touchscreen tablets have found their way into classrooms, as well. In many private schools, students are required to have one, and the school loads it with software and materials needed for course curricula. In Europe, an Icelandic company, InfoMentor, provides a cloud-based learning platform for schools in several countries that can be accessed on any device—computers, touchscreen tablets, and smartphones—by teachers, students, and parents.

In the United States, the fastest growing company for products and services bringing touchscreen tablets into schools is Amplify, a subsidiary of News Corporation, one of the world's largest media conglomerates. Its platform provides independent learning and focuses on the skills required by Common Core State Standards (CCSS). Pupils progress at their own pace, lessons have gamelike qualities with immediate feedback, and the programs provide comprehensive data on each student's progress.

Data collection is the double-edged sword that divides those for and against these programs. Data is necessary to improve both a student's performance and program effectiveness. But parents are concerned that pupil-tracking software invades their children's privacy. They're wary of large, for-profit firms having access to details about their child's school activities and learning history.

These programs are new. Objective, well-controlled research that measures a range of outcomes, not just test scores, are yet to be conducted. Safeguards for children's privacy need to be addressed. Ironically, more data is needed.

KEEP THE LINES OF COMMUNICATION OPEN

Whatever direction your child's school is taking to use technology in the classroom, it does not replace our responsibility as parents to guide our child's use of it at home. To do this, we need to stay connected with our children, as they connect with the next new thing.

By the time you read this, who knows what the latest games, most popular social networking sites, or most useful productivity apps and browser extensions will be? What's important is that you spend time getting to know the ones that matter to your child and that you keep up an ongoing, age-appropriate dialogue with your child about them.

Encourage intelligent conversation about innovation in technology. For instance, ask questions such as, "Is faster always better?" or "Is a way of doing something always preferable because it's new?"

Encourage critical thinking. It's surprising how many smart kids rely on the Internet indiscriminately and are easily misled. In the hundreds of hours I've spent researching this book, I've come across many facts and findings. Here's the scariest one:

- In the United States, "39% of kids, ages 9 to 17, agree with the statement: 'The information I find online is always correct.'"[16]

The future lies in the hands of our children, and they need adult guidance.

This concludes the seven steps to teach your child to pay attention. In the next chapter we'll cover some topics of special interest. We'll look at research that supports both pros and cons of popular screen activities and get some insights into self-control that can help your child keep attention snatchers in check.

PART THREE

Your Child's Future

Chapter 11 takes a closer look at some popular attention snatchers, including video gaming, social media, and television. It also discusses what science tells us about helping kids build their mental muscle for self-control. Chapter 12 returns us to the heart of parenting—raising our children to be strong and free.

11

Paying Attention to Attention

When I was growing up, my parents told me, "Finish your dinner. People in China and India are starving." I tell my daughters, "Finish your homework. People in India and China are starving for your job."

—Thomas Friedman

In this chapter, we'll discuss topics of special interest and frontiers of research in children's attention. We'll also look at what science tells us about how to help kids build self-control.

SOME PROS AND CONS OF VIDEO GAMES

For eons, educators have recognized that effective learning is active, goal-oriented, contextualized, and interesting—which turn out to be the exact attributes of video games. Educational games, at home and at school, teach specific content, such as language arts, math, and science. But children learn from popular off-the-shelf video games, too—genres such as action, strategy, and role-playing. (Violent content of video games is an important and controversial issue, but it's not the focus of this book, and this section doesn't include research findings in this area.)

Most studies that show mental gains from playing video games have been conducted with young adults, but children most likely receive the same benefits. Research shows that playing certain types of video games improves similar types of perceptual skills,[1] spatial skills,[2] and cognitive skills,[3] as measured by computerized tests of these abilities. Here, we'll look specifically at video games and attention.

Laboratory Measures of Attention. Research links action games, such as *Halo*, *Medal of Honor*, and *Doom*, with improved onscreen allocation of attention.[4] In shooter games, a player focuses on targets, ignoring irrelevant distractions on the screen. Action-game players get significantly better scores on computerized assessments of attention, such as the test of variables in attention (TOVA).[5] On the TOVA, shapes appear on a computer screen. Subjects respond as fast as they can when they see a shape in a target location, but not when it appears elsewhere on the screen.

Action-game players do better at computerized-object-tracking tasks and also demonstrate less "attentional blink," the tendency to miss a second target on a screen if it's presented 180 to 450 milliseconds after the first one.[6]

One study included children. Subjects were seventy-five non-action-game players and fifty-six action-game players, ages seven to twenty-two years old. Action-game players did better on the attention network test (ANT), which measures reaction time to computerized tasks of alerting, orienting, and noticing incongruencies on a screen.[7]

Attention at School. The other side of the bitcoin is that video games are designed to become habit-forming. It's a selling point for game makers. By necessity, if your child increases the amount of time he spends gaming, he decreases the amount of time he does other things—for example, physical exercise or homework. Economists call this "opportunity cost," or the value of the best alternative foregone. Also, your child may lose patience for activities that have less sensory stimulation.

Researchers have established a link between time spent playing action video games and decreased grade-point average for eighth and ninth graders.[8] A two-year study of third- to eighth-grade "pathological" gamers (a term that we'll discuss shortly) showed that they represented 9 percent of gamers and had significantly lower grades in school.[9] A national study of eight- to eighteen-year-old children showed that 8 percent were pathological gamers and had significantly lower grades and significantly more attention problems at school.[10]

Studies that link increased gaming and inattention at school don't prove that habitual gaming *causes* these attention problems. To do this, experimenters would need to randomly assign children to play or not play video games for lengthy periods of time, and then compare them on measures of attention at school, which ethically they cannot do. Instead, when scientists study behaviors that have been linked to potentially harmful results, such as lower grades and less attention at school, they do so by analyzing data as it exists in the world. They identify links or correlations that are statistically significant—in other words, extremely unlikely to occur by chance. Then, since a preexisting attention problem might be the cause of both the increased gaming and the inattention at school, researchers statistically control for attention problems children had prior to the study. Results are then more likely due to increased gaming.

One such study of grade-schoolers and adolescents showed that as video game playing and TV watching increased, so did attention problems in the classroom. Significant results included teachers' reports of not "staying on task," not "paying attention," and "interrupting other children's work."[11] In other studies, for adolescents, gaming for more than one hour per weekday was associated with significantly more subsequent attention problems,[12] and gaming for more than one hour per day was associated with a significant worsening of ADHD symptoms.[13]

In 2010, a rare, randomized, controlled study of children's video gaming and inattention at school was conducted. The subjects were boys, ages six to nine years old, who did not yet own video consoles. Experimental subjects received a console and three games at the outset of the study. A comparable control group received no console until the end of the four-month study period.

Parents recorded their sons' activities from the end of the school day until bedtime. Teachers reported their attention-related behavior in class. Pre- and post-tests of reading and writing were administered. During the four months, the boys with the gaming consoles spent significantly less time after school reading and studying, and after the four months, had significantly more difficulties with attention at school and significantly lower scores in reading and writing.[14] (It's possible that after the first four months some of the boys would start to play less, but some might play more, too.)

Because of the results, it was deemed unethical to conduct another randomized, controlled study like this one with children. It would probably be impossible now anyway, to find enough six- to nine-year-old boys who don't already play video games.

In Step Six (chapter 8), we discussed multigenerational video gaming. If it were ethical to replicate the 2010 randomized, controlled study—it's not, nor should it be—I'd want to add an additional experimental group: children whose parents play, discuss gaming, and set limits with them. What might the results be then? With the right attitude, metacognition, and honest communication, could parents help kids integrate a reasonable amount of gaming into their young lives without loss to their academics?

AZEROTH BECKONS

Some pioneering educators are exploring the potential benefits of massively multiplayer online role-playing games (MMOs, MMORs, or MMORPGs) in the classroom. In an MMO, players take on the identity of heroes engaged in a quest. In this type of game environment, when you try something new, failure is anticipated, so students can develop a mind-set conducive to creative problem-solving. These educators use a popular MMO called *World of Warcraft* (*WoW*) to motivate students in reading, writing, and other academics. Students are taught to apply gaming strategies to solve real-world problems, cooperate with others in a learning community, and adapt the mind-set of being heroes in their own lives.

The curriculum began as an after-school program but has been implemented as a language-arts elective. The founders are building a "*World of Warcraft* in School" (or "MMO-School") wiki for interested teachers. (A "wiki" is a collaborative website to which anyone can contribute or edit material. For example, *Wikipedia* is a wiki encyclopedia.)

Student engagement and work samples suggest that the program is beneficial, but gathering hard evidence is a challenge. As soon as assessment is introduced, students lose their freedom to fail and recover. Plus, the question of what we're *not* looking at needs to be addressed. Does increased screentime for a game with a constant level of high sensory stimulation have unintended consequences? What are its effects on students' voluntary attention outside of this class?

World of Warcraft (*WoW*) takes place in mythical Azeroth, where two factions exist: the Alliance and the Horde. Each faction consists of races, such as humans, gnomes, and trolls. A player chooses a faction and a race, and then a class, such as shaman, warlock, or hunter. Players can form groups and guilds to meet challenges and organize events. For example, a hunting party consists of five players who are different characters with different specialized skill sets. Each player needs to further his own expertise and also needs to work with others who have different expertise needed for the quest.

In the real world, the counterpart to a *WoW* group is the cross-functional team—a workgroup of specialists in different areas who need to collaborate to complete a project. Could *WoW* be a training ground for corporate teambuilding? *Wired* ran a story about the hiring of a senior manager at Yahoo who was a guild master in *WoW*. It concluded, "The day may not be far off when companies receive résumés that include a line reading 'level 60 tauren shaman in *World of Warcraft*.'"[15] But what about the number of hours that go into achieving level 60?

Although subscriptions have declined in the past several years with the introduction of MMOs that don't require one, in 2008, *WoW* had over 11 million subscribers who spent an average of twenty-three hours per week playing.[16] As incidents of players neglecting their real-world responsibilities hit the news, "World of Warcrack" became a slang term, replacing "Evercrack," the slang term for *Everquest*, the popular MMO that preceeded it.

IS INTERNET ADDICTION REAL?

More than 6 million video gamers in China spend at least twenty-two hours per week playing; more than 10 million in the United Kingdom, France, and Germany spend at least twenty hours per week playing; and, as previously mentioned, more than 5 million in the United States play an average of forty-five hours per week.[17] But experts say that excessive gaming is not the same as pathological gaming.

In the United States, the official reference for psychiatric diagnosis is the *Diagnostic and Statistical Manual of Mental Disorders, Fifth Edition: DSM-5*.[18] After much debate, this edition, published in 2013, includes only one behavioral (nonsubstance) addiction, gambling disorder, as a formally diagnosable condition. It includes Internet gaming disorder in a section called "Conditions for Further Study," acknowledging that persistent, recurrent gaming can result in serious impairment or distress.

Prior to making this decision, an American Psychiatric Association workgroup reviewed over 250 publications on the prevalence, course, treatment, and biomarkers of Internet gaming disorder. They stated that they were unable to reach conclusions because the studies used different criteria to define the disorder. To help standardize the definition, the *DSM-5* lists nine criteria, derived from the reports that the workgroup reviewed.

In addition to significant impairment or distress, to fulfill the definition of Internet gaming disorder, five of nine criteria must be met.[19] The criteria are as follows:

- Preoccupation with games
- Withdrawal symptoms, such as irritability, anxiety, or sadness

- A high level of tolerance for gaming
- Unsuccessful attempts to stop or limit gaming
- Loss of interest in other activities
- Continued excessive use despite knowing it's a problem
- Deceiving others about the amount of time spent gaming
- Use of gaming to escape or relieve a bad mood
- Jeopardizing or losing a significant relationship, job, or educational opportunity

Much of the scientific literature that the *DSM-5* workgroup reviewed is from Asian countries. The workgroup visited a hospital in China where Internet gaming disorder is a recognized addiction. In 2007, the Chinese government ordered computer game operators to set up a "game fatigue system." It encourages minors to play less than three hours per day by reducing their points in the game and by issuing periodic warnings: "You have entered unhealthy game time, please go offline immediately to rest."[20]

South Korea, a world leader in its early and widespread use of broadband, now considers Internet addiction to be one of its most serious public health issues. According to data from 2006, approximately 210,000 South Korean children—or 2.1 percent of children ages six to nineteen years of age—needed treatment. Between 20 and 25 percent of them required hospitalization. Treatment includes medication, group sessions, and brain-wave monitoring.[21] By 2007, South Korea had trained 1,043 counselors in the treatment of Internet addiction, enlisted over 190 hospitals as treatment centers, and introduced preventive measures to be taught in schools.[22]

From preschool to high school in South Korea, students now learn about the dangers of Internet addiction. Kindergarteners are taught to control how long they stay online. Preschoolers sing songs with lyrics that instruct them to close their eyes and stretch their bodies after playing computer games. They read stories about children who become addicted but then remember how to play without using a screen.[23]

Researchers say that it's easier to study the problem in Asia, where Internet cafés are frequently used, as compared to the United States, where "attempts to measure the phenomenon are clouded by shame, denial, and minimization."[24] In online forums here, gamers say that dependence on gaming is a problem only for those with addictive personalities who develop unhealthy gaming habits. The popular term is "pathological gaming," and the popular sentiment is "It's about the person, not the game."

As previously mentioned, in the United States approximately 8 to 9 percent of children who play video games are considered to be pathological gamers. As we discussed in chapter 3, some children are born with temperaments that predispose them toward high levels of sensory stimulation and action. But when it comes to a behavior like gaming, a child's biology is not his destiny. A child's brain is still growing and being shaped as a result of interacting with his environment.

"Addictive personality" is a loosely defined, poorly understood term that can cause harm if applied to children. It puts them at risk for a self-fulfilling prophecy. If it helps you be more vigilant and firm in setting limits, think of your child as being a dopamine-driven kid who tends to go to extremes. If your child finds it harder to walk away from his favorite video game than most of the other kids do, he needs more structure and guidance from you than most of the other kids need from their parents. Help him use strategies to stop, as skillfully as he uses strategies to play. Also, keep in mind, that children without a genetic predisposition can develop a dependency on video gaming. Pay close attention to how quickly and how strongly your child's gaming habits grow.

If your child has developed a serious habit, consult your health care professional. You can get more information at On-Line Gamers Anonymous (Olganon.org).

ADHD AND VIDEO GAMING

The link between ADHD and increased risk for substance abuse and pathological gambling—sometimes called the "dopamine connection"—is well established. ADHD has also been identified as a risk factor for compulsive gaming. In one prospective study, two thousand adolescents were followed for two years. ADHD was found to be the most significant predictor of Internet addiction.[25]

Children with ADHD are particularly vulnerable to the immediacy and variability of feedback and high sensory stimulation of video games. Gaming puts minimal demands on skills like patience, listening, and slowing down, which are more difficult for children with ADHD.

A child with ADHD tends to seek enhanced stimulation of reward pathways in the brain.[26] Video gaming has been shown to increase dopamine release, activating these pathways.[27] Many parents are surprised the first time they turn off a device in the middle of a game and their child flies into a rage. They abruptly turned off the dopamine valve and their child's brain is fighting reactively to get it turned back on.

Experts postulate that ADHD symptoms and gaming addiction share a "bidirectional relationship." In other words, ADHD symptoms make gaming attractive, and gaming exacerbates symptoms. When a child with ADHD games too much, he's continually reinforcing impulsive, rapid, hyperfocused reactivity, neglecting reading, playing sports, and face-to-face interactions that develop emotional self-control and voluntary attention without a screen.[28] His symptoms worsen, except when he's gaming, so it's a relief for everyone for him to keep gaming.

When this occurs, it's a daunting challenge for parents to try to restore balance. Have honest, age-appropriate conversations with your child about the risk factors he needs to manage. Frame your discussion in positive terms. As we discussed in chapter 3, kids with ADHD are "hunters." They need purposeful "big game" in the real world to pursue instead of video game goals in the virtual world. Help your child find his island of competence (as we discussed in Step Four, chapter 7) and look for teachable moments to help him strengthen his self-control.

SOCIAL MEDIA AND THE RISE OF CASUAL GAMES

Social media has much to offer, especially to teens who use it to retain friendships, grapple with social norms, explore interests, develop technical skills, and experiment with new forms of self-expression.[29]

How does your child use social media? The latest upsurge in social networking is casual or mobile gaming. Sometimes dubbed "gaming for nongamers," these simple, easy-to-play games post scores and invitations to play through newsfeeds and messages. Popular games include *Farmville, Cityville, Angry Birds, Temple Run, Candy Crush Saga*, and more. Some have their own sites, but most are embedded in Facebook. That way, you can share scores, ask your friends for more lives, or receive requests to access new levels.

Because casual games are simple to learn and easy to play, they're often a multitasker's online activity of choice. They can be played on handheld devices, anytime, anywhere. If a teacher, an assembly, or a phone conversation is boring, your teen can use the time to raise her score on her favorite game. Then she doesn't feel like she's wasting time. The immediate high-stim rewards create the sensation that she's making progress.

According to a 2012 trend report from Newzoo (a gaming market research company), young people are powering the casual game movement.[30] Young adults (ages twenty-two to thirty-five) represent 53 percent of casual gamers, which means casual gaming could be impacting toddlers. Weary parents may be getting a much-needed lift from playing, but this is a critical time when parents' faces and voices are getting imprinted in their babies' brains. Babies are primed to respond to human faces. They thrive on parents' undivided attention.

Adolescents (ages ten to twenty years old) make up 25 percent of casual gamers, and their dopamine-sensitive teen brains make them prime candidates to get hooked. Casual games have short levels and give frequent bursts of victory. Dopamine is released at quick, variable intervals through the reward centers of their brains.

As we discussed in Step Six (chapter 9), multigenerational gaming is helpful, and this applies to casual games, too. When playing with your child, have fun but also use teachable moments to deconstruct games. Identify what makes them alluring and discuss their economic profitability. The casual games market is estimated to be an $8.64 billion industry.[31]

OVERCOMING FOMO (FEAR OF MISSING OUT)

Instant communication, especially social media, distorts our perception of where we stand in the social order. Kids feel this acutely. They're constantly ranking themselves along dimensions such as looks, popularity, and wit. Kids rarely post an unflattering picture of themselves online. They take selfies with popular kids at parties or at the mall. And so, in the middle of every ordinary day of their lives, kids see the highlights of the lives of others, which makes their lives seem dull by comparison.

This is why "FOMO," the fear of missing out, is on the rise. *New York Times* reporter Jenna Wortham calls it "emblematic of the digital age."[32] FOMO kicks up feelings of inadequacy, anxiety, and agitation. Adults get it, too. Suddenly, we're full of self-doubt, wondering, "Why does their family have more friends than we do?" "How come they know how to live and we don't?" "How come their kids are always smiling and ours look so bored?"

Recently, a preschool teacher told me that neither she nor the other teachers at her school liked having iPads in their classrooms. They got touchscreen tablets, though, because parents were afraid that the absence of them in the classroom would leave their children unprepared for kindergarten—specifically, uncompetitive with other preschoolers who were using iPads to learn. Preschool is an important time for children to interact and learn how to get along with others. Placing touchscreen tablets in preschool is a question that needs to be approached cautiously. Choosing an answer based on a fear that's evoked by the imagined future academic success of other preschoolers using iPads is letting FOMO make that decision for you.

The way to prevent FOMO—or at least hold it in check—is with awareness and metacognition: asking the question, "What am I *not* thinking about?" What are *my* priorities? When you overcome your own FOMO, you make better decisions as a parent and you also set a good example for your children.

Encourage your kids to keep social networking in perspective and appreciate the value of face-to-face contact. A collective realization in our culture is growing about this. In April 2014, a five-minute video by Gary Turk titled "Look Up" was posted on YouTube. Within a week, it had 26 million views and twelve thousand comments. Within a month, it had 40 million views and thirty-two thousand comments. The spoken-word video begins with the writer-director looking into the camera and saying,

> I have 422 friends
> Yet I'm lonely.

It shows how much we can lose by letting screens trap our attention involuntarily instead of giving voluntary attention to real-world relationships. It's a good video to watch with your child and discuss the reasons why it instantly went viral.

TV, MOVIES, AND VIDEOS

The most passive form of digital media is TV.

Toddlers and Preschoolers. Research has shown that viewing entertainment television before age three is significantly associated with attention problems at age seven, and the magnitude of this association is large.[33] But even a very strong correlation does not prove causation. Although unlikely, the toddlers could already have had attention problems. Some toddlers gravitate to TV more than others do, and it's believed that they may have a genetic predisposition for high-sensory stimulation.[34] While we can't do much about an inclination that a child is born with, we can limit the amount of TV she watches and also what she's watching—especially if a child shows early signs of being at risk for weak voluntary attention.

Research has shown that preschoolers can learn from educational programs such as *Sesame Street*,[35] but not all programs labeled as educational have positive effects. For example, one study showed that *Dora the Explorer*, *Clifford*, and *Arthur* were linked with improvements in language development, but that the show *Teletubbies* was linked with decrements. After analyzing the effects of TV shows on preschoolers, the study found that educational programs must engage the preschooler, elicit direct participation, model language proficiently, avoid overloading the child with distracting stimulation, and include a well-articulated narrative framework.[36]

Grade-Schoolers. Watching TV is associated with attention difficulties and lower academic achievement in grade-schoolers, in both high-income and low-income school districts.[37] These effects are enduring. In a long-term prospective study of 1,037 children in New Zealand, television-viewing times were obtained from parents when children were five, seven, nine, and eleven years of age. Teacher-reported attention problems were obtained when the children were thirteen and fifteen years old. The mean number of hours of TV watching in childhood was directly related to attention problems in adolescence. These results remained significant after statistically controlling for attention problems in early childhood, which means that increased screentime most likely caused the increased attention problems.[38]

Teens. In a similar study in the United States, families were interviewed when their children were ages fourteen, sixteen, and twenty-two years old. Frequent television viewing by adolescents was associated with higher risk for subsequent attention difficulties. TV watchers had significantly more incomplete homework, poor grades, and long-term academic failure. These results also remained significant after statistically controlling for prior attention problems, suggesting that TV viewing was not just a link but a cause.[39]

As parents, we may think we have a good grasp on the pull of television because we grew up with TV, too. But movies and TV today have higher production values, faster action, and more spectacular special effects than ever. As kids, we didn't have hundreds of channels in high definition on a giant flat-screen with surround sound that makes us feel like we're in a movie theater. Nor could we download any movie or TV show instantly on a tablet or smartphone, or click on a link to a video that a friend just posted, tweeted, or texted.

Watching TV, movies, and videos has a place, to be sure. They're terrific for families to view together and enjoy. They can help your child learn about a wide variety of subjects—history, geography, natural science, current events, how to dance or design clothes or cook.

Help your child learn to intentionally watch TV by selecting programs beforehand. A DVR can help kids make shows fit their schedules, not vice versa, and it also minimizes ads. Keep an eye on what your child is watching and if something pops up that you feel needs an explanation, talk it over with her. The same holds true for admirable content, such as characters who are good role models. Let your child know who you like on TV and why.

Choose your child's movies with care. Movies vividly tell stories, and stories teach children what it's like to be human. As mythologist and psychologist Joseph Campbell eloquently put it, "Stories show us how to bear the unbearable, approach the unapproachable, conceive the inconceivable. Stories provide meaning, texture, layers and layers of truth."

Movies can inspire kids in ways that can last. A 2014 report in the *Economist* on advances in the design of robots observed, "There was very little academic research in robotics before there were undergraduates who had seen *Star Wars* as kids.[40]

STRENGTHENING YOUR CHILD'S SELF-CONTROL

Remember the four-year-olds in the marshmallow test we discussed in chapter 1? They were more successful at resisting the hot stimulus when they put it out of sight than when they stared at it. Our best strategy to resist a screen is to put it away and get involved in something else. But screens are ubiquitous and that wears down our willpower.

Research psychologist Roy Baumeister has conducted a series of experiments that show that the more we're exposed to any one temptation, the less able we are to resist any of them. For example, subjects who spent time in a room resisting a hot stimulus such as chocolate later scored poorly on tasks of persistence, as compared to control subjects who did not endure the chocolate temptation.[41]

Baumeister calls this principle "ego depletion." His research has demonstrated that our capacity for willpower is exhaustible and works much like a muscle. If we exercise our willpower, eventually, it grows strong, but each time we exercise it, we hit a stopping point. We run out of glucose, the brain's fuel for mental exertion.[42]

Ego depletion helps to explain the very real challenge our children face carrying screens with them wherever they go. They constantly need to resist temptation, so they use up their reserve of willpower. Ego depletion explains how they come to be controlled by their technology, instead of them controlling it.

In Step Two (chapter 5), we discussed "background tech"—keeping a digital device in view even though it's not in use. As ego depletion predicts, the presence of a device on a table or a shelf slowly erodes your child's resolve. If instead, you keep it in a drawer or a purse, although that is less convenient, you help your child preserve her self-control. This is especially true for a preschooler, who is particularly susceptible. Eventually the drawer or purse will come to represent the phone or iPad to your child, and the strategy will lose much of it effectiveness. Then, you'll need to vary where you conceal your digital devices. The

American Academy of Pediatrics recommends no televisions in children's bedrooms and no smartphones at the dinner table, either.[43]

A friend told me recently that she took her seven-year-old daughter and a friend on an overnight camping trip, and she allowed them to bring their iPads. She thought it would help settle them down at night in the tent. She pictured technology-free fun in nature all day, and then a cozy time at night, snuggling in sleeping bags in the glow of an iPad. What happened was that the kids knew the iPad was with them, and they couldn't stop themselves from asking for it every time there was a momentary lull. If they hadn't known an iPad was there, they'd have felt freer to explore their surroundings and get into their adventure.

It's hard to say no to our children, but it's in those very moments that we help them learn self-control. For example, if your child asks if she can have a TV in her room, you've got a teachable moment. Talk with her about how saying yes would be easier for you, too—it would keep her busy and eliminate arguments about the family TV. But, in the big picture, it's not good for her self-control and that's a higher priority for her success in life.

Researchers have shown that a person's belief moderates the way that ego depletion takes place. Reduced self-control after a demanding task is greater in those who believe that they've become less able to resist temptation.[44] These findings have important implications for parents. They mean that the belief you have in your child's ability to resist attention snatchers is a strong determining factor in her actual ability to do so.

One other line of research in self-control worth mentioning is about the way we justify indulging ourselves.[45] When we feel we've worked hard or we receive feedback that we've done well, we tend to feel that we deserve a reward. We're more apt to give in to a hot stimulus. This is also true if we feel we've been deprived. The implications here are, as we've previously discussed, to avoid both gratuitous praise for children and overly strict rules. As we discussed in chapter 1, our goal is to balance our yin and yang.

THE TRIUMPH OF VOLUNTARY ATTENTION

In *How Children Succeed*, author Paul Tough emphasizes the need for cultivating self-control and "grit" or perseverance in children. He recounts the words of Jonathan Rowson, a grand master of chess, who said, "When it comes to ambition, it is crucial to distinguish between 'wanting' something and 'choosing' it."

If all you do is *want* something, he explains, you'll inevitably fail to put in the necessary hard work. If you *choose* it, then you will "reveal your choice through your behavior and your determination. Every action says, 'This is who I am.'"[46]

Choose to raise children who have self-control. And teach them to choose self-control for themselves. If they say they want a better grade in school, ask them if they *choose* it. Then, when it's time to decide between a screen and a book, ask them which one they *choose*.

In the next and final chapter, we'll look at your authority as a parent to protect the promise of your child's future.

12

The Power of Parenthood

There are only two lasting bequests we can hope to give our children. One of these is roots, the other, wings.

—Johann Wolfgang von Goethe

Jack Andraka, age seventeen, is a medical entrepreneur. At age fifteen, he developed a revolutionary sensor strip to detect early-stage pancreatic cancer that costs three cents per test, takes five minutes to run, and is close to 100 percent accurate. "My research would definitely not have been possible in the pre-Internet stage," says Andraka. "I have all the world's information at my fingertips."[1]

As parents, we carry with us the knowledge that our children, for better or worse, have all the world's information at their fingertips. Will they, like Andraka, use it for the better, to fulfill themselves and contribute to our world?

BELIEVE IN YOUR CHILD

Recently, I was talking to a mom who was describing the slumber parties her eight-year-old daughter and her friends have. Each girl brings a digital device and they all play the same game at the same time. *Fashion Designer* and *Cupcake Maker* are popular right now. In *Fashion Designer*, they put together head-to-toe outfits trying new combinations of color and style. With *Cupcake Maker*, they choose flavors and decorations.

The other mom and I laughed as we fondly recalled pre-high-tech slumber parties when girlfriends played dress-up or hung out in the kitchen and baked. Eight-year-old girls can still do that, too, but right now they're having a blast instantly transforming their ideas into images and sharing their creations with each other. It's not the way we did things, but these are their slumber parties, not ours. I'm reminded of the words of John F. Kennedy: "For time and the world do not stand still. Change is the law of life." And also those of Yogi Berra, "The future ain't what it used to be."

It can be hard to trust in your child's future when you discover him on Snapchat in the middle of the night or quickly clearing the cache on his browser when you walk into the room. Yet, your child's belief in himself starts with your belief in your child.

If your child has attention problems, is going through a rough patch, or is just not a cookie-cutter kid, it's difficult to watch him struggle. You may feel helpless, but there's one thing you can do that will make a difference. You can continue to believe in him and his future. When comedian Stephen Colbert accepted his Emmy in 2013, he reminded us of the power of parents. Can you imagine the quick-witted Colbert as a pupil in school? "I want to thank my mom," he said, "for not worrying about me and believing I'd be OK."

UNDERSTAND THE NATURE OF YOUR OWN AUTHORITY

In 2012, the ninth most popular video on YouTube was "Facebook Parenting."[2] A dad sits in a chair facing a camera and reads a printout of his fifteen-year-old daughter's Facebook post from which he had been blocked. In it, his daughter gripes, in graphic language, about her chores. Then, the dad addresses her complaints, also in graphic language. After that, he stands up, takes out a .45-caliber pistol, and fires nine rounds of bullets into his daughter's computer.

"Facebook Parenting" has nearly 40 million views and has been featured in national media—on *20/20*, the *Today Show*, and more. Viewers still post heated comments either applauding or denouncing the dad.

This entire father-daughter exchange took place onscreen, with no in-person contact. The daughter posted to Facebook and the father to YouTube. While extreme, it represents a dynamic that's creeping into our culture—avoidance of face-to-face encounters and the civility that accompanies them.

It's emotionally difficult to face a person who is important in your life—your child or your parent—and work through the inevitable misunderstandings that occur in everyday life. The inner tension of feeling we need to set something straight is what gets us to do it. But now, with instant diversions, we can ignore that inner tension, or even channel it into online drama instead. Issues remain unresolved and are prone to escalate.

We need to remember that as parents, we're the ones who can foresee long-term consequences and we need to act accordingly. We are the grown-ups.

Another popular video on YouTube, "A Magazine Is an iPad That Does Not Work,"[3] is both funny and instuctive. This video starts out with a one-year-old gleefully using an iPad. Then we see her placing her fingers on photos in magazines in the exact same manner. It's evident that she's trying to get a response from them, but the pictures don't move. In a final frame, using text on a screen, the parent observes that for her daughter, a magazine is an iPad that doesn't work. "It will remain so her whole life," the parent notes. "Steve Jobs has coded a part of her OS."

The parent's comments are insightful in a number of ways. First, she's able to see the world through her baby daughter's eyes. Also, she appreciates that brain pathways forming now will endure. But what do you think about her final comment?

Chances are, this parent is just trying to bring a smile to our faces, and maybe compliment Jobs for making the iPad so intuitive. But her comment does remind me of a sentiment I've heard from many other parents of young children—a kind of resignation that they don't have much influence as parents when it comes to their children's consumption of digital media.

As we've discussed throughout this book, the difference between voluntary and involuntary attention is crucial, and we're becoming more imbalanced toward involuntary attention, which is a passive act. We allow our children's attention to be captured, and we allow our sense of control over that to be captured, too. But we can't become passive. It's up to us, as adults, to see what's happening and do what it takes to restore balance.

By the way, isn't it delightful that this preverbal one-year-old is testing a hypothesis completely on her own? That's not the result of having all the world's information at her fingertips. That's the result of her curiosity and the mystery and marvel that is a young child's brain.

RAISING CHILDREN TO FLY STRONG AND FREE

There is a fable about a bird and a fox. One day, the fox offers the bird a worm in exchange for a single feather. "Oh, good" says the bird. "I don't have to wake up early, dig deep, and pull one up myself. And I won't miss just one feather. I have so many to spare." The bird accepts the worm, gives the fox a feather, and happily flies away. The next day, the fox appears again with the same offer. Again, the bird agrees, recalling with pleasure the easy trade he'd made. This happens again the following day, and the day after that, and for days after that. Then one day, after the trade, the bird tries but can no longer fly, and the fox eats him for dinner.

When our kids give in to the call of their screens to be entertained just for today, the effects are negligible, as they are for the bird who won't miss just one feather. But if children grow up, day after day, avoiding the work of building their voluntary attention without cues from a screen, they'll be limited by their weak attention and get swallowed up by this world.

Strengthening voluntary attention and the brain pathways that support it requires effort. There are no deals that can be made with the fox that don't end badly. That's why parenting in the age of attention snatchers requires awareness, knowledge, and balance.

You are your child's first teacher, most important authority figure, and persuasive presence during his formative years. Don't be intimidated by your child's adeptness with digital media. Your child needs you now, more than ever. When children build strong voluntary attention, no matter what task they face or what tempts them, their wings will be sturdy and they'll fly strong and free.

Notes

If you're copying a URL from this section into your browser, leave out the period at the end. It's not part of the Web address and may result in a 404 page-not-found error.

When a doi was available for a journal article or an abstract, I included it. A doi is a digital object identifier. If a document is moved from one website to another, a doi will find the new site for you. (You'll always be able to find a runaway bunny.)

INTRODUCTION

1. As a result of numerous, well-controlled studies that document its effectiveness, cognitive-behavioral therapy (CBT) is recognized as a first-line, evidence-based treatment for anxiety and depression in children and adults. See Andrew Butler et al., "The Empirical Status of Cognitive-Behavioral Therapy: A Review of Meta-Analyses," *Clinical Psychology Review* 26 (2006): 17–31; and Stefan G. Hofmann et al., "The Efficacy of Cognitive Behavioral Therapy: A Review of Meta-Analyses," *Cognitive Therapy Research* 36 (2012): 427–440.
2. American Psychiatric Association, *Diagnostic and Statistical Manual of Mental Disorders, Fifth Edition: DSM-5* (Washington, D.C.: American Psychiatric Association, 2013).

CHAPTER 1: A PARENT'S DILEMMA

1. David Pogue, "A Parent's Struggle with a Child's iPad Addiction," *New York Times*, February 24, 2011, http://pogue.blogs.nytimes.com/2011/02/24/a-parents-struggle-with-a-childs-ipad-addiction/. Pogue's son was using *Puppet Pal* to create animated cartoon shorts; *Easy Beats* to compose complex rhythms; *Cut the Rope*, a physics-based puzzle; and *Rush Hour*, a game of strategy. His post drew 929 comments that day.
2. Hanna Rosen, "The Touchscreen Generation," *Atlantic*, April 2013, 56–65.
3. Jonah Lehrer, "Don't! The Secret of Self-Control," *New Yorker*, May 18, 2009. Summarizes the original Stanford marshmallow experiment and the follow-up studies that tracked subjects from age four to age forty. Also explains how attention is the key to self-control, the parts of the brain and dopamine pathways that are involved, and how self-control of attention is taught to students in certain charter schools, which have shown dramatic improvement in inner-city students' test scores.

   To observe children in settings that replicate Mischel's experimental paradigm, enter the search term "marshmallow test" on YouTube. These video clips provide an entertaining appreciation of children's efforts to refrain from eating treats when left alone in a room.

   For the original studies, see Walter Mischel, Ebbe Ebbesen, and Antoinette Zeiss, "Cognitive and Attentional Mechanisms in Delay of Gratification," *Journal of Personality and Social Psychology* 21 (1972): 204–218, doi:10.1037/h0032198; Walter Mischel, Yuichi Shoda, and Philip J. Peake, "The Nature of Adolescent Competencies Predicted by Preschool Delay of Gratification," *Journal of Personality and Social Psychology* 54 (1988): 687–696, http://bingschool.stanford.edu/pub/wmischel/108-JPSP%201988.pdf; Walter Mischel, Yuichi Shoda, and Monica L. Rodriguez, "Delay of Gratification in Children," *Science* 244 (1989): 933–938, doi:10.1126/science.2658056; Walter Mischel et al., "'Willpower' over the Life Span: Decomposing Self-Regulation," *Social Cognitive and Affective Neuroscience* 6 (2011): 252–256, doi:10.1093/scan/nsq081; and Tanya Schlam, "Preschoolers' Delay of Gratification Predicts Their Body Mass 30 Years Later," *Journal of Pediatrics* 162 (2013): 90–93, doi:10.1016/j.jpeds.2012.06.049.

4. Walter Mischel, *The Marshmallow Test: Mastering Self-Control* (New York: Little, Brown, 2014).
5. Angela L. Duckworth and Martin Seligman, "Self-Discipline Outdoes IQ in Predicting Academic Performance of Adolescents," *Psychological Science* 16 (2005): 939–944, doi:10.1111/j.1467-9280.2005.01641.x. A longitudinal study of eighth-graders in Pennsylvania that shows how cognitive control (voluntary attention) was twice as influential as IQ in predicting future grades and admissions to selective high schools.
6. Terrie E. Moffitt et al., "A Gradient of Childhood Self-Control Predicts Health, Wealth, and Public Safety," *Proceedings of the National Academy of Sciences,* 108 (2011): 2693–2698, doi:10.1073/pnas.1010076108. Report on the Dunedin Multidisciplinary Health and Development Study, which tracked 1,037 New Zealanders and found that direct observation and measures of cognitive control (voluntary attention) at ages three to eleven predicted physical health, financial success, and freedom from addiction and societal misconduct at age thirty-two.
7. Daniel Kahneman, *Thinking Fast and Slow* (New York: Farrar, Straus & Giroux, 2013).
8. Steven Fleming, "Relating Introspective Accuracy to Individual Differences in Brain Structure," *Science* 329 (2010): 1541–1543, doi:10.1126/science.1191883. Describes the neural basis of metacognition.
9. Nancy Carlsson-Paige, quoted in Valerie Strauss, "Is Technology Sapping Children's Creativity?" *Washington Post*, September 13, 2012. Carlsson-Paige's quotation is from her acceptance speech for a lifetime achievement award from the Robert F. Kennedy Children's Action Corps.

CHAPTER 2: WHAT IS VOLUNTARY ATTENTION?

1. Michael I. Posner and Steven E. Peterson, "The Attention System of the Human Brain," *Annual Review of Neuroscience* 13 (1990): 25–42. The most widely cited article in brain research on attention. Posner's tripartite "network of attention" is organized by function, neurochemistry, and brain anatomy: (1) alerting (alarm response; norepinephrine; brain stem arousal; and right hemisphere) and (2) orienting (response to sensory events; cholinergic; parietal lobe) are involuntary.

In contrast, (3) executive function (effortful control; dopamine; midline frontal–anterior cingulate cortex) is voluntary.

2. Daniel Goleman, *Focus* (New York: Harper, 2013). Describes involuntary and voluntary attention by the names of their corresponding neural pathways, "bottom-up" and "top-down." In Daniel Kahneman, *Thinking Fast and Slow* (New York: Farrar, Straus & Giroux, 2013), these systems are described as "System 1" and "System 2." Both books offer more information about these systems and are written for the general public.
3. Maria Nordfang, Mads Dyrholm, and Claus Bundessen, "Identifying Bottom-Up and Top-Down Components of Attentional Weight by Experimental Analysis and Computational Modeling," *Journal of Experimental Psychology* 142 (2013): 510–535, doi:10.1037/a0029631. Explains how stimuli compete for neural representation. A stimulus "wins" because its features produce the most energy, due to contingencies of the moment, referred to as "attentional weight."
4. Steven E. Peterson and Michael Posner, "The Attention System of the Brain: 20 Years After," *Annual Review of Neuroscience* 35 (2012): 73–89, doi:10.1146/annurev-neuro-062111-150525. After two decades of brain-imaging research, including an estimated five thousand imaging papers on attention, Posner published an update of his definitive 1990 review (see note 1 for this chapter), which had been based primarily on behavioral studies, now confirmed by the new brain-imaging evidence.

   Also see Gordon L. Shulman and Maurizio Corbetta, "Two Attentional Networks: Identification and Function within a Larger Cognitive Architecture," in *Cognitive Neuroscience of Attention,* 2nd ed., ed. Michael Posner (New York: Guilford Press, 2011).
5. Glyn W. Humphreys and Eirini Mavritsaki, "Models of Visual Search: From Abstract Function to Biological Constraint," in *Cognitive Neuroscience of Attention,* 2nd ed., ed. Michael Posner (New York: Guilford Press, 2011). Found evidence of parietal lobe suppression when subjects successfully ignored distracting visual stimuli.
6. Fumi Katsuki and Christos Constantinidis, "Bottom-Up and Top-Down Attention: Different Processes and Overlapping Neural Systems," *Neuroscientist*, December 20, 2013, doi:10.1177/1073858413514136.

7. Bjorn H. Schott et al., "Mesolimbic Functional Magnetic Resonance Imaging Activations during Reward Anticipation Correlate with Reward-Related Ventral Striatal Dopamine Release," *Journal of Neuroscience* 28 (2008): 14311–14319, doi:10.1523/jneurosci.2058-08.2008.
8. National Institutes of Health, "The Teen Brain: Still under Construction," National Institute of Mental Health publication, available in hard copy or pdf download at www.nimh.nih.gov/health/publications/the-teen-brain-still-under-construction.
9. B. J. Casey et al., "Behavioral and Neural Correlates of Delay of Gratification 40 Years Later," *Proceedings of the National Academy of Sciences* 108 (2011): 14998–15003, doi:10.1073/pnas.1108561108. High-delayers showed greater neural activity in their prefrontal cortex; low-delayers showed greater activity in their ventral striatum.

CHAPTER 3: YOUR CHILD'S AMAZING BRAIN

1. Carl Zimmer, "100 Trillion Connections: New Efforts Probe and Map the Brain's Detailed Architecture," *Scientific American*, January 2011, 19.
2. Mary K. Rothbart et al., "Developing Mechanisms of Self-Regulation in Early Life," *Emotion Review* 3 (2011): 207–213, doi:10.1177/1754073910390565.
3. Nina Auerbach, "Kindergarten Readiness," School of Education at Johns Hopkins University: New Horizons for Learning, http://education.jhu.edu/PD/newhorizons/lifelonglearning/early-childhood/kindergarten-readiness.

   The National Center for Educational Statistics that Auerbach cites are from the Early Childhood Longitudinal Study.
4. John R. Best and Patricia H. Miller, "A Developmental Perspective on Executive Function," *Child Development* 81 (2010): 1641–1660, www.ncbi.nlm.nih.gov/pmc/articles/PMC3058827/.
5. Young Adult Development Project, at the Massachusetts Institute of Technology Center for Work, Family and Personal Life, http://hrweb.mit.edu/worklife/youngadult/brain.html.
6. Katherine Sharpe, "Hyper One Day, Calm the Next," *Scientific American Mind*, March–April 2011, 10.

7. Philip Shaw et al., "Attention-Deficit/Hyperactivity Disorder Is Characterized by a Delay in Cortical Maturation," *Proceedings of the National Academy of Sciences* 104 (2007): 19649–19654, doi:10.1073/pnas.0707741104. A longitudinal study comparing cortical thickness at more than 40,000 cerebral points on each of 824 MRI scans of 223 children with ADHD and 223 controls, at time intervals, an average of 2.8 years apart. Results showed thickness at median age 10.5 years for ADHD children comparable to thickness at median age 7.5 years for controls. The delay was most prominent in prefrontal regions, where children with ADHD reached their peak thickness approximately 5 years after normally developing controls.
8. Norman Doidge, *The Brain That Changes Itself* (New York: Penguin Books, 2007).
9. Cecilia Wahstedt, Lisa B. Thorell, and Gunilla Bohlin, "Heterogeneity in ADHD: Neuropsychological Pathways, Comorbidity, and Symptom Domains," *Journal of Abnormal Child Psychiatry* 37 (2009): 551–564, doi:10.1007/s10802-008-9286-9.
10. Philip Shaw et al., "Trajectories of Cerebral Cortical Development in Childhood and Adolescence and Adult Attention-Deficit/Hyperactivity Disorder," *Biological Psychiatry* 74 (2013): 599–606, doi:10.1016/j.biopsych.2013.04.007.
11. Jessica J. M. Barnes et al., "The Molecular Genetics of Executive Function: Role of Monoamine System Genes," *Biological Psychiatry* 69 (2011): 127–143, doi:10.1016/j.biopsych.2010.12.040. Evidence from cognitive neuroscience and pharmacology implicates dopamine, norepinephrine, and serotonin as the neurochemicals that mediate executive functions. A review of gene variance related to these neurochemicals showed some association with individual differences in sustained attention but less for response inhibition and self-observation.
12. E. Wang et al., "The Genetic Architecture of Selection at the Human Dopamine Receptor D4 (DRD4) Gene Locus," *American Journal of Human Genetics* 74 (2004): 931–944, doi:10.1086.420854.
13. Stephen V. Faraone et al., "Meta-Analysis of the Association between the 7-Repeat Allele of the Dopamine D4 Receptor Gene and Attention Deficit Hyperactivity Disorder," *American Journal of Psychiatry* 158 (2001): 1052–1057, doi:10.1176/appi.ajp.158.7.1052.

14. Yuan-Chun Ding et al., "Evidence of Positive Selection Acting at the Human Dopamine Receptor D4 Gene Locus," *Proceedings of the National Academy of Sciences* 99 (2002): 309–314, doi:10.1073/pnas.012464099.
15. E. Wang et al., "The Genetic Architecture of Selection at the Human Dopamine Receptor D4 (DRD4) Gene Locus," *American Journal of Human Genetics* 74 (2004): 931–944, doi:10.1086/420854. In the words of the principal investigator: "Resource-depleted, time-critical, or rapidly changing environments might select for individuals with 'response-ready' adaptations, whereas resource-rich, time-optimal, or little-changing environments might select against such adaptations."
16. David Dobbs, "Restless Genes," *National Geographic*, January, 2013, 45–57.
17. Thomas Hartmann, *Attention Deficit Disorder: A Different Perception* (Novato, Calif.: Underwood-Miller, 1993).
18. Lucy Jo Palladino, *The Edison Trait* (New York: Times Books, 1997); republished in paperback as *Dreamers, Discoverers, and Dynamos* (New York: Ballantine, 1999).
19. Centers for Disease Control and Prevention, "Attention Deficit / Hyperactivity Disorder (ADHD) Data and Statistics," www.cdc.gov/ncbddd/adhd/data.html. The gradual increase in prevalence was as follows: 7.8 percent in 2003; 9.5 percent in 2007; 11.0 percent in 2011.
20. Charles Duhigg, *The Power of Habit* (New York: Random House, 2012).

CHAPTER 4:
STEP ONE: GET INTO THE RIGHT MIND-SET

1. "Generation M2: Media in the Lives of 8- to 18-Year-Olds," Henry J. Kaiser Family Foundation, January 20, 2010, http://kff.org/other/event/generation-m2-media-in-the-lives-of/.
2. Mary K. Rothbart et al., "Developing Mechanisms of Self-Regulation in Early Life," *Emotion Review* 3 (2011): 207–213, doi:10.1177/1754073910387943.

CHAPTER 5: STEP TWO: BE THE CHANGE YOU WANT TO SEE IN YOUR CHILD

1. Timothy D. Wilson et al., "Just Think: The Challenge of the Disengaged Mind," *Science* 345 (2014): 75–77, doi:10.1126/science.1250830.
2. Albert Bandura, Dorothea Ross, and Sheila A. Ross, "Transmission of Aggression through Imitation of Aggressive Models," *Journal of Abnormal and Social Psychology* 65 (1961): 575–582, http://psychclassics.yorku.ca/Bandura/bobo.htm.
3. Giacomo Rizzolatti and Laila Craighero, "The Mirror-Neuron System," *Annual Review of Neuroscience* 27 (2004): 169–192. This is a technical article. For an informative, plain-language presentation, visit *Nova* at PBS (air date January 25, 2005), www.pbs.org/wgbh/nova/body/mirror-neurons.html.
4. M. E. Schmidt et al., "The Effects of Background Television on the Toy Play Behavior of Very Young Children," *Child Development* 79 (2008): 1137–1151.
5. G. Blake Armstrong and Bradley S. Greenberg, "Background Television as an Inhibitor of Cognitive Processing," *Human Communication Research* 16 (1990): 355–386, doi:10.1111/j.1468-2958.
6. Matthew A. Lapierre, Jessica T. Piotrowski, and Deborah L. Linebarger, "Background Television in the Homes of U.S. Children," *Pediatrics* 130 (2012): 839–846, doi:10.1542/peds.2011-2581.
7. Perri Klaus, "Parents, Wired to Distraction," *New York Times,* March 10, 2014, http://well.blogs.nytimes.com/2014/03/10/parents-wired-to-distraction.

CHAPTER 6: STEP THREE: PRACTICE THE 3 RS OF GOOD ATTENTION

1. Gretchen Reynolds, "How Physical Fitness May Promote School Success," *New York Times*, September 18, 2013, http://well.blogs.nytimes.com/2013/09/18/how-physical-fitness-may-promote-school-success.
2. John J. Ratey, *Spark: The Revolutionary New Science of Exercise and the Brain* (New York: Little, Brown, 2008).

3. Archer Trevor and Richard M. Kostrzewa, "Physical Exercise Alleviates ADHD Symptoms: Regional Deficits and Development Trajectory," *Neurotoxicity Research* 21 (2012): 195–209, doi:10-10007/s12640-011-9260-0.
4. R. R. Rauner et al., "Evidence That Aerobic Fitness Is More Salient Than Weight Status in Predicting Standardized Math and Reading Outcomes in Fourth- through Eighth-Grade Students," *Journal of Pediatrics* 163 (2013): 344–348, doi:10.1016/j.jpeds.2013.01.006.
5. H. Guiney and L. Machado, "Benefits of Regular Aerobic Exercise for Executive Functioning in Healthy Populations," *Psychonomic Bulletin Review* 20 (2013): 73–86, doi:10.3758/s13423-012-0345-4.
6. Lew Hardy et al., *Understanding Psychological Preparation for Sport: Theory and Practice of Elite Performers* (Hoboken, N.J.: John Wiley, 1996).
7. *Special Health Report from Harvard Medical School: Understanding Depression* (Cambridge, Mass.: Harvard Health Publications, 2013). Excerpt titled "Exercise and Depression" available online at www.health.harvard.edu/newsweek/Exercise-and-Depression-report-excerpt.htm.
8. World Health Organization, *Global Strategy on Diet, Physical Activity, and Health* (Geneva, Switzerland: WHO Press, 2010).
9. Richard Louv, *Last Child in the Woods* (New York: Algonquin Books, 2008).
10. Richard Louv, *The Nature Principle* (New York: Algonquin Books, 2012).
11. Frances E. Kuo and A. Faber Taylor, "A Potential Natural Treatment for Attention-Deficit/Hyperactivity Disorder: Evidence for a National Study," *American Journal of Public Health* 94 (2004): 1580–1586, www.ncbi.nlm.nih.gov/pmc/articles/PMC1448497/.
12. Andrea Fabor Taylor and Frances E. Kuo, "Children with Attention Deficits Concentrate Better after Walk in the Park," *Journal of Attention Disorders* 12 (2009): 402–409, doi:10.1177/1087054708323000.
13. National Center for Education Statistics, *Digest of Education Statistics, 2011* (Washington, D.C.: U.S. Department of Education, 2012). The critical reading average score for the SATs in 2010–2011 (497) was 8 points lower than in 1998–1999.
14. "Louis C.K. Hates Cell Phones," on *Conan*, the Conan O'Brien late-night talk show, http://youtu.be/5HbYScltf1c.

15. Stephen Covington, *Seven Habits of Highly Effective People* (New York: Simon and Schuster, 1989).
16. Susan Cain, *Quiet* (New York: Broadway Books, 2013).
17. Sendhl Mullainathan and Eldar Sharif, *Scarcity* (New York: Penguin Books, 2013).
18. A. Chiesa and A. Serretti, "A Systematic Review of Neurobiological and Clinical Features of Mindfulness Meditations," *Psychological Medicine* 40 (2010): 1239–1252, doi:10.1017/S0033291709991747.

    See also: Judson A. Brewer et al., "Mindfulness Training for Smoking Cessation: Results from a Randomized Trial," *Drug and Alcohol Dependence* 119 (2011): 72–80, doi:10.1016/j.drugalcdep.2011.05.027; Daphne M. Davis and Jeffrey A. Hayes, "What Are the Benefits of Mindfulness? A Practice Review of Psychotherapy-Related Research," *Psychotherapy* 48 (2011): 198–208, www.apa.org/pubs/journals/features/pst-48-2-198.pdf; Norman A. Farb et al., "Attending to the Present: Mindfulness Meditation Reveals Distinct Neural Modes of Self-Reference," *Social Cognitive and Affective Neuroscience* 4 (2007): 313–323, doi:10.1093/scan/nsm030; B. K. Holzel et al., "Mindfulness Leads to Increases in Regional Brain Gray Matter Density," *Psychiatry Research* 191 (2011): 36–43, www.ncbi.nlm.nih.gov/pmc/articles/PMC3004979/; Yi-Yuan Tang et al., "Short-Term Meditation Induces White Matter Changes in the Anterior Cingulate," *Proceedings of the National Academy of Science* 107 (2010): 15649–15652, doi:10.1073/pnas.1011043107.
19. Sharon Begley, *Train Your Mind, Change Your Brain* (New York: Ballantine Books, 2007). A readable review of the initial research findings on the positive effects of meditation on brain plasticity, with a foreword by the Dalai Lama.
20. Jon Kabat-Zinn, *Full Catastrophe Living*, rev. ed. (New York: Bantam, 2013).
21. Major research findings compiled by the University of Massachusetts Medical School, Center for Mindfulness in Medicine, Health Care and Society, www.umassmed.edu/cfm/research/publications.
22. "Mindfulness with Jon Kabat-Zinn," at Google, October 11, 2007 (over 2 million views as of 2014), http://youtu.be/3nwwKbM_vJc.
23. William Kuyken et al., "Effectiveness of the Mindfulness in Schools Programme: Non-Randomized Controlled Feasibility Study," *British Journal of Psychiatry*, June 20, 2013, doi:10.1192/bjp.bp.113.126649.

See also: C. Burke, "Mindfulness-Based Approaches with Children and Adolescents: A Preliminary Review of Current Research in an Emergent Field," *Journal of Child and Family Studies* 19 (2010): 133–144, doi:10.1007/s10826-009-9282-x; L. Flook et al., "Effects of Mindful Awareness Practices on Executive Functions in Elementary School Children," *Journal of Applied School Psychology* 26 (2010): 70–95, doi:10.1080/15377900903379125; M. Klatt et al., "Feasibility and Preliminary Outcomes for Move-Into-Learning: An Arts-Based Mindfulness Classroom Intervention," *Journal of Positive Psychology* 8 (2013): 133–241, doi.10.1080/17439760.2013.779011; E. M. Sibinga et al., "Mindfulness-Based Stress Reduction for Urban Youth," *Journal of Alternative and Complementary Medicine* 17 (2011): 213–218, www.ncbi.nlm.nih.gov/pmc/articles/PMC3157305/.

24. David Hochman, "Mindfulness: Getting Its Share of Attention," *New York Times*, November 1, 2013, www.nytimes.com/2013/11/03/fashion/mindfulness-and-meditation-are-capturing-attention.
25. Maryanne Wolf, *Proust and the Squid: The Story and Science of the Reading Brain* (New York: HarperCollins, 2007).
26. Nicholas Carr, *The Shallows: What the Internet Is Doing to Our Brains* (New York: W. W. Norton, 2010).
27. Nicolas Carr, "Is Google Making Us Stupid?" *Atlantic Monthly,* July–August, 2008, www.theatlantic.com/magazine/archive/2008/07/is-google-making-us-stupid/306868/.
28. *Kids and Family Reading Report*, 3rd ed., 2010. Research conducted by the Harrison Group and published by Scholastic. Download available at http://mediaroom.scholastic.com/research.
29. Carol Dweck, *Mindset: The New Psychology of Success* (New York: Random House, 2006).
30. Letitia Stein, "U.S. Pediatricians Urge Reading Aloud to Children from Birth," *Reuters*, June 24, 2014, www.reuters.com/article/2014/06/25/us-usa-children-read-idUSKBN0F000520140625.
31. *Kids and Family Reading Report*, 4th ed., 2012. Research conducted by the Harrison Group and published by Scholastic. Download available at http://mediaroom.scholastic.com/kfrr.
32. "Louis C.K. Hates Cell Phones," on *Conan*, the Conan O'Brien late-night talk show, http://youtu.be/5HbYScltf1c.

CHAPTER 7: STEP FOUR: TURN UP REAL-WORLD HAPPINESS

1. Robert Brooks and Sam Goldstein, *Raising Resilient Children* (New York: McGraw-Hill, 2002).
2. Jane McGonigal, *Reality Is Broken* (New York: Penguin Press, 2011).

CHAPTER 8: STEP FIVE: THINK LIKE A CHILD, ACT LIKE A PARENT

1. American Academy of Pediatrics, "AAP Health Initiatives: Media and Children," www.aap.org/en-us/advocacy-and-policy/aap-health-initiatives/pages/media-and-children.aspx.
2. Daniel Goleman, *Emotional Intelligence* (New York: Bantam Books, 1995).
3. Lucy Jo Palladino, *Find Your Focus Zone* (New York: Free Press, 2007).
4. American Academy of Pediatrics, "AAP Health Initiatives: Media and Children," www.aap.org/en-us/advocacy-and-policy/aap-health-initiatives/pages/media-and-children.aspx.
5. "Facebook and Your Privacy," *Consumer Reports*, June 2012, www.consumerreports.org/cro/magazine/2012/06/facebook-your-privacy/index.htm.
6. Danah Boyd et al., "Why Parents Help Their Children Lie to Facebook about Age," *First Mind* 16 (2011), http://journals.uic.edu/ojs/index.php/fm/article/view/3850/3075.
7. David Dobbs, "Beautiful Brains," *National Geographic,* October 2011, http://ngm.nationalgeographic.com/2011/10/teenage-brains/dobbs-text. See also National Institutes of Health, "The Teen Brain: Still under Construction," National Institute of Mental Health publication, available in hard copy or pdf download at www.nimh.nih.gov/health/publications/the-teen-brain-still-under-construction.
8. Daniel J. Siegel, *Brainstorm: The Power and Purpose of the Teenage Brain* (New York: Tarcher, 2013).
9. Pew Research Center, "Video Games Galore," May 26, 2009, www.pewresearch.org/daily-number/video-gamers-galore/.
10. Jane McGonigal, *Reality Is Broken* (New York: Penguin Press, 2011).
11. Edward L. Swing et al., "Television and Video Game Exposure and

the Development of Attention Problems," *Pediatrics*, July 5, 2010, doi:10.1542/peds.2009-1508.

12. Phillip A. Chan and Terry Rabinowitz, "A Cross-Sectional Analysis of Video Games and Attention Deficit Hyperactivity Disorder Symptoms in Adolescents," *Annals of General Psychiatry* 5 (2006), doi:10.1186/1744-859X-5-16.
13. Mental Health Advisory Team 6, Operation Enduring Freedom 2009, Afghanistan, November 6, 2009, Section 6.2, "Individual Coping Behaviors," 33–34, http://timemilitary.files.wordpress.com/2012/07/mhat_vi-oef_redacted.pdf.
14. Laura M. Holson, "Text Generation Gap: U R 2 Old (JK)," *New York Times*, March 9, 2008.
15. John Cline, "The Mystery of Deep Sleep," *Psychology Today*, October 11, 2010, www.psychologytoday.com/blog/sleepless-in-america/201010/the-mystery-deep-sleep.
16. U.S. Centers for Disease Control and Prevention, "Sleep and Sleep Disorders," July 1, 2013, www.cdc.gov/sleep/about_sleep/how_much_sleep.htm.
17. Larry Rosen, "To Sleep . . . Perchance to Reset Your Brain," *National Psychologist*, July–August 2012, 12.
18. Stephani Sutherland, "Bright Screens Could Delay Bedtime," *Scientific American Mind*, January 2013, www.scientificamerican.com/article/bright-screens-could-delay-bedtime.
19. Daniel L. King et al., "The Impact of Violent Video-Gaming on Adolescent Sleep: An Experimental Study," *Journal of Sleep Research* 22 (2013): 137–143, doi:10.1111/j.1365-2869.2012.01060.x.
20. Catherine Steiner-Adair, *The Big Disconnect* (New York: HarperCollins, 2013).
21. Drew Guarini, "9 Ways Video Games Can Actually Be Good for You," *Huffington Post*, November 7, 2013, www.huffingtonpost.com/2013/11/07/video-games-good-for-us_n_4164723.html.
22. James C. Rosser Jr. et al., "The Impact of Video Games on Training Surgeons in the 21st Century," *JAMA Surgery* (formerly *Archives of Surgery*) 142 (2007): 181–186, doi:10.1001/archsurg.142.2.181.
23. Domenico Giannotti et al., "Play to Become a Surgeon: Impact of Nintendo Wii Training on Laparoscopic Skills," *PLOS One*, February 27, 2013, doi:10.1371/journal.pone.0057372.

24. Association of American Medical Colleges, "FACTS: Applicants, Matriculants, Enrollment, Graduates, MD/PhD, and Residency Applicants Data," www.aamc.org/data/facts/.
25. David Elkin, *The Hurried Child*, 3rd ed. (New York: Perseus Publishing, 2001).

CHAPTER 9:
STEP SIX: BECOME A FOCUS-FRIENDLY FAMILY

1. U.S. Centers for Disease Control and Prevention, "Sleep and Sleep Disorders," July 1, 2013, www.cdc.gov/sleep/about_sleep/how_much_sleep.htm.
2. Po Bronson, "Snooze or Lose," *New York Magazine*, October 7, 2007, http://nymag.com/news/features/38951/.
3. Avi Sadeh, Reut Gruber, and Amiram Raaviv, "The Effects of Sleep Restriction on School-Age Children: What a Difference an Hour Makes," *Child Development* 74 (2003): 444–455, doi:10.1111/1467-8624.7402008.
4. Amy R. Wolfson and Mary A. Carskadon, "Sleep Schedules and Daytime Functioning in Adolescents," *Child Development* 69 (1998): 875–887, doi:10.1111/j.1467-8624.1998.tb06149.x.
5. Judith A. Owens, "A Clinical Overview of Sleep and Attention-Deficit/Hyperactivity Disorder in Children and Adolescents," *Journal of the Canadian Academy of Child and Adolescent Psychiatry* 18 (2009): 92–102, www.ncbi.nlm.nih.gov/pmc/articles/PMC2687494/.

   See also E. J. Paavonenm, T. Porkka-Heiskanen, and A. R. Lahikainen, "Sleep Quality, Duration, and Behavioral Symptoms among 5–6-Year-Old Children," *European Child and Adolescent Psychiatry* 18 (2009): 747–754, doi:10.1007/s00787-009-0033-8.
6. V. Sung et al., "Sleep Problems in Children with Attention-Deficit/Hyperactivity Disorder: Prevalence and the Effect on the Child and Family," *JAMA Pediatrics* (formerly *Archives of Pediatric and Adolescent Medicine*) 162 (2008): 336–342, doi:10.1001/archpedi.162.4.336.
7. J. Biederman and T. Spencer, "Attention-Deficit/Hyperactivity Disorder (ADHD) as a Noradrenergic Disorder," *Biological Psychiatry* 46 (1999): 1234–1242, www.ncbi.nlm.nih.gov/pubmed/10560028.
8. S. Cortese et al., "Sleep in Children with Attention-Deficit/Hyperac-

tivity Disorder: Meta-Analysis of Subjective and Objective Studies," *Journal of the American Academy of Child and Adolescent Psychiatry* 48 (2009): 894–908, doi:10.1097/chi.0b013e3181ac09c9.

9. A. M. Wood, "Gratitude Influences Sleep through the Mechanism of Pre-Sleep Cognitions," *Journal of Psychosomatic Research* 66 (2009): 43–48, doi:10.1016/j.jpsychores.2008.09.002.
10. Eliza Cook and Rachel Dunifon, "Parenting in Context: Do Family Meals Really Make a Difference?" Cornell University College of Human Ecology, www.human.cornell.edu/pam/outreach/upload/Family-Mealtimes-2.pdf.
11. Lori Takeuchi and Reed Stevens, "The New Coviewing: Designing for Learning through Joint Media Engagement," Joan Ganz Cooney Center, December 8, 2011, www.joanganzcooneycenter.org/publication/the-new-coviewing-designing-for-learning-through-joint-media-engagement.
12. "Move Over Monopoly: ASU Researchers Find Families Bond over Video Game Play," *ASU News: Business, Culture, and Affairs*, July 9, 2013, https://asunews.asu.edu/20130709_families_video games.
13. Sarah Coyne et al. "Game On . . . Girls: Associations between Co-Playing Video Games and Aolescent Behavioral and Family Outcomes," *Journal of Adolescent Health* 49 (2011): 160–165, doi:10.1016/j.jadohealth.2010.11.249.
14. Cynthia Chiong, "Can Video Games Promote Intergenerational Play and Literacy Learning?" Joan Ganz Cooney Center, March 22, 2010, www.joanganzcooneycenter.org/publication/can-video-games-promote-intergenerational-play-literacy-learning.
15. Jordan Shapiro, "Why Playing Video Games Makes You a Better Dad," *Forbes*, November 15, 2012, www.forbes.com/sites/jordanshapiro/2012/11/15/why-playing-video-games-makes-you-a-better-dad.
16. Marc G. Berman, John Jonides, and Stephen Kaplan, "The Cognitive Benefits of Interacting with Nature," *Psychological Science* 19 (2008): 1207–1212, doi:10.1111/j.1467-9280.2008.02225.x.
17. Heather Ohly et al., "Attention Restoration Theory: A Systematic Review of the Attention Restoration Value of Natural Environments," University of Exeter Medical School, European Centre for Environment and Human Health (2014), www.ecehh.org/research-projects/attention-restoration-theory-a-systematic-review/.

CHAPTER 10: STEP SEVEN: CELEBRATE SUCCESS BUT PREPARE FOR STRONGER SNATCHERS

1. Larry Rosen, "Welcome to the iGeneration," *Psychology Today*, March 26, 2010, www.psychologytoday.com/blog/rewired-the-psychology-technology/201003/welcome-the-igeneration. Based on Nielson Company data.
2. Ryan Fleming, "Oculus Rift Has Sold over 85,000 Prototypes," *Digital Trends*, April 16, 2014, www.digitaltrends.com/gaming/oculus-rift-sold-85000-prototypes/#!Gdnbp.
3. Cameron Robinson, "5 Amazing Non-Game Uses for Oculus-Rift," *Reality Check*, January 19, 2014, http://youtu.be/MNAa_QI_jbA.
4. "Grandmother Uses Oculus Rift as Therapy," http://youtu.be/o5eI HyFYFMM.
5. Eric Limer, "I Wore the New Oculus Rift and I Never Want to Look at Real Life Again," *Gizmodo*, January 7, 2014, http://gizmodo.com/i-wore-the-new-oculus-rift-and-i-never-want-to-look-at-1496569598.
6. Carmen Nobel, "Neuromarketing: Tapping into the 'Pleasure Center' of Consumers," *Forbes,* February 1, 2013, www.forbes.com/sites/hbsworkingknowledge/2013/02/01/neuromarketing-tapping-into-the-pleasure-center-of-consumers.
7. Gregory S. Berns and Sara E. Moore, "A Neural Predictor of Cultural Popularity," *Journal of Consumer Psychology* 22 (2012): 154–160, doi:10.1016/j.jcps.2011.05.001.
8. Michael Moss, *Salt, Sugar, Fat* (New York: Random House, 2013).
9. John Gaudiosi, "News Reports Forecast Global Videogame Industry Will Reach $82 Billion by 2017," *Forbes:* July 18, 2012, www.forbes.com/sites/johngaudiosi/2012/07/18/new-reports-forecasts-global-video-game-industry-will-reach-82-billion-by-2017/.
10. Jennifer Levitz, "Makers Fight Efforts to Study Link to Violence," *Wall Street Journal*, December 10, 2013.
11. Brian Solomon, "Facebook Buys Oculus, Virtual Reality Gaming Startup, for $2 Billion," *Forbes*, March 25, 2014, www.forbes.com/sites/briansolomon/2014/03/25/facebook-buys-oculus-virtual-reality-gaming-startup-for-2-billion/.
12. "Habbo Hotel—Where Else?" *Sulake*, www.sulake.com/habbo.

13. Kahn Academy, www.khanacademy.org.
14. "*A* Is for Algorithm," *Economist*, April 26–May 2, 2014.
15. Matt Richtel, "Reading, Writing, Arithmetic, and Lately, Coding," *New York Times*, May 10, 2014.
16. *Kids and Family Reading Report*, 3rd ed., 2010. Research conducted by the Harrison Group and published by Scholastic. Download available at http://mediaroom.scholastic.com/research.

CHAPTER 11: PAYING ATTENTION TO ATTENTION

1. Matthew W. G. Dye, C. Shawn Green, and Daphne Bavelier, "Increasing Speed of Processing with Action Video Games," *Current Directions in Psychological Science* 18 (2009): 321–326, doi:10..1111/j.1467-8721.2009.01660.x.
2. C. Shawn Green and Daphne Bavelier, "Learning, Attentional Control, and Action Video Games," *Current Biology* 22 (2012): 197–206, doi:10.1016/j.cub.2012.02.012.

   See also D. H. Uttal et al., "The Malleability of Spatial Skills: A Meta-Analysis of Training Studies," *Psychological Bulletin* 139 (2013): 352–402, doi:10.1037/a0028446; and S Kühn et al., "Playing Super Mario Induces Structural Brain Plasticity: Gray Matter Changes Resulting from Training with a Commercial Video Game," *Molecular Psychiatry* 19 (2014), 265–271, doi:10.1038/mp.2013.120.
3. C. Shawn Green et al., "The Effect of Action Video Game Experience on Task-Switching," *Computers in Human Behavior* 28 (2012): 984–994, doi:10.1016/j.chb2011.12.020.

   See also Brian D. Glass, W. Todd Maddox, and Bradley C. Love, "Real-Time Strategy Game Training: Emergence of a Cognitive Flexibility Trait," *Plos One*, August 7, 2013, doi:10.1371/journal.pone.0070350.
4. Isabela Granic et al., "The Benefits of Playing Video Games," *American Psychologist* 69 (2014): 66–78, doi:10.1037/a0034857.
5. Matthew W. G. Dye, C. Shawn Green, and Daphne Bavelier, "Increasing Speed of Processing with Action Video Games," *Current Directions in Psychological Science* 18 (2009): 321–326, doi:10..1111/j.1467-8721.2009.01660.x.

6. Walter R. Boot et al., "The Effects of Video Game Playing on Attention, Memory, and Executive Control," *Acta Psychologica* 129 (2008): 387–396, doi:10.1016/j.actpsy.2008.09.005.
7. Matthew W. G. Dye, C. Shawn Green, and Daphne Bavelier, "The Development of Attention Skills in Action Video Game Players," *Neuropsychologica* 47 (2009): 1780–1789, doi:10.1016/j.neuropsychologia.2009.02.002.
8. Douglas A. Gentile, "The Effects of Violent Video Game Habits on Adolescent Hostility, Aggressive Behaviors, and School Performance," *Journal of Adolescence* 27 (2004): 5–22, doi:10.1016/j.adolescence.2003.10.002.
9. Douglas A. Gentile et al., "Pathological Video Game among Youths: A Two-Year Longitudinal Study," *Pediatrics* 127 (2011): 319–329.
10. Douglas A. Gentile et al., "Pathological Video-Game Use among Ages 8 to 18," *Psychological Science* 20 (2009): 594–602, doi:10.1111/j.1467-9280.2009.02340.x.
11. Edward L. Swing et al., "Television and Video Game Exposure and the Development of Attention Problems," *Pediatrics* 126 (2010): 214–221, doi:10.1542/peds.2009-1508.
12. Edward L. Swing et al., "Television and Video Game Exposure and the Development of Attention Problems," *Pediatrics* 126 (2010): 214–221, doi:10.1542/peds.2009-1508.
13. Phillip A. Chan and Terry Rabinowitz, "A Cross-Sectional Analysis of Video Games and Attention Deficit Hyperactivity Disorder Symptoms in Adolescents," *Annals of General Psychiatry* 5 (2006), doi:10.1186/1744-859X-5-16.
14. Robert Weis and Brittany Cerankowsky, "Effects of Video-Game Ownership on Young Boys' Academic and Behavioral Functioning: A Randomized, Controlled Study," *Psychological Science* 21 (2010): 463–470, doi:10.1177/0956797610362670.
15. John Seely Brown and Douglas Thomas, "You Play *World of Warcraft*? You're Hired!" *Wired*, April 2006, http://archive.wired.com/wired/archive/14.04/learn.html.
16. Jessica Trybus, "Game-Based Learning: What It Is, Why It Works, and Where It's Going," National Media Institute, www.newmedia.org/game-based-learning--what-it-is-why-it-works-and-where-its-going.html.

17. Jane McGonigal, *Reality Is Broken* (New York: Penguin Books, 2011).
18. American Psychiatric Association, *Diagnostic and Statistical Manual of Mental Disorders, Fifth Edition: DSM-5* (Washington, D.C.: American Psychiatric Association, 2013).
19. Nancy M. Petry and Charles P. O'Brien, "Internet Gaming Disorder and the *DSM-5*," *Addiction* 108 (2013): 1186–1187, doi:10.1111/add.12162.
20. "Internet Addiction around the World," *Frontline*, PBS, February 2, 2010, www.pbs.org/wgbh/pages/frontline/digitalnation/virtual-worlds/internet-addiction/internet-rescue-camp.html.
21. Jan Schiller, "New Laws and Clinic to Combat Internet Addiction in South Korea," *Kotaku*, June 23, 2011, http://kotaku.com/5814878/new-laws-and-clinic-to-combat-internet-addiction-in-south-korea.
22. Jerald J. Block, "Issues for *DSM-V*: Internet Addiction," *American Journal of Psychiatry* 165 (2008): 306–307, doi:10.1176/appi.ajp.2007.07101556.
23. Youkyung Lee, "South Korea: 160,000 Kids between Age 5 and 9 Are Internet-Addicted," *Huffington Post*, November 28, 2012, www.huffingtonpost.com/2012/11/28/south-korea-internet-addicted_n_2202371.html.
24. Jerald J. Block, "Pathological Computer Use in the U.S.," in *International Symposium on the Counseling and Treatment of Youth Internet Addiction* (Seoul: National Youth Commission, 2007), 433.
25. C. H. Ko et al., "Predictive Values of Psychiatric Symptoms for Internet Addiction in Adolescents: A 2-Year Prospective Study," *JAMA Pediatrics* (formerly *Archives of Pediatric and Adolescent Medicine*) 163 (2009): 937–943, doi:10.1001/archpediatrics.2009.159.
26. N. D. Volkow et al. "Evaluating Dopamine Pathways in ADHD; Clinical Implications," *Journal of the American Medical Association* 302 (2009): 1084–1091, doi:10.1001/jama.2009.1308.
27. M. J. Koepp, "Evidence for Striatal Dopamine Release during a Video Game," *Nature* 393 (1998): 266–268, doi:10.1038/30498.
28. Margaret D. Weiss et al., "The Screens Culture: Impact on ADHD," *Attention Deficit and Hyperactivity Disorders* 3 (2011): 327–334, doi:10.1007/s12402-011-0065-z.
29. Mizuko Ito et al., "Living and Learning with New Media: Summary of Findings from the Digital Youth Project," November, 2008, http://

digitalyouth.ischool.berkeley.edu/files/report/digitalyouth-TwoPage-Summary.pdf.

30. "Casual and Social Games Trends Report," Newzoo, February 28, 2012, www.newzoo.com/trend-reports/casual-social-games-trend-report/.
31. Jason Evangelho, "2012's Massive Casual Gaming Footprint," *Forbes*, January 2, 2013, www.forbes.com/sites/jasonevangelho/2013/01/02/2012s-massive-casual-gaming-footprint-is-the-hardcore-audience-disappearing/.
32. Jenna Wortham, "Feel Like a Wallflower? Maybe It's Your Facebook Wall," *New York Times*, April 10, 2011.
33. Frederick Zimmerman and Dimitri Chistakis, "Associations between Content Types of Early Media Exposure and Subsequent Attentional Problems," *Pediatrics* 120 (2007): 986–992, doi:10.1542/ped.2006-3322.
34. Carlin Miller et al., "Brief Report: Television Viewing and Risk for Attention Problems in Preschool Children," *Journal of Pediatric Psychology* 32 (2007): 448–452, doi:10.1093/jpepsy/jsl035.
35. Daphne Bavalier, C. Shawn Green, and Matthew W. G. Dye, "Children, Wired—For Better or Worse," *Neuron* 67 (2010): 692–701, doi:10.1016/j.neuron.2010.08.035.
36. Deborah L. Linebarger and Dale Walker, "Infants' and Toddlers' Television Viewing and Language Outcomes," *American Behavioral Scientist* 48 (2005): 624–645, doi:10.1177/0002764204271505.
37. Elif Ozmert, Muge Toyran, and Kadriye Yurdakok, "Behavioral Correlates of Television Viewing in Primary School Children Evaluated by the Child Behavior Checklist," *JAMA Pediatrics* (formerly *Archives of Pediatric and Adolescent Medicine*) 156 (2002): 910–915, www.ncbi.nlm.nih.gov/pubmed/12197799.
38. Carl Erik Landhuis et al., "Does Childhood Television Viewing Lead to Attention Problems in Adolescence? Results from a Prospective Longitudinal Study," *Pediatrics* 120 (2007): 532–537, doi:10.1542/peds.2007-0978.
39. Jeffrey G. Johnson et al., "Extensive Television Viewing and the Development of Attention and Learning Difficulties during Adolescence," *Pediatrics* 161 (2007): 214–221, doi:10.1542/peds.2009-1508.

40. "Immigrants from the Future: Special Report on Robots," *Economist*, March 29–April 4, 2014, 10.
41. Roy F. Baumeister et al., "Ego Depletion: Is the Active Self a Limited Resource?" *Journal of Personality and Social Psychology* 74 (1998): 1252–1265, doi:10.1037/0022-3514.74.5.1252.
42. Roy F. Baumeister and John Tierney, *Willpower: Rediscovering the Greatest Human Strength* (New York: Penguin Books, 2012).
43. "How to Make a Family Media Use Plan," *American Academy of Pediatrics*, December 3, 2013, www.healthychildren.org/English/family-life/Media/Pages/How-to-Make-a-Family-Media-Use-Plan.aspx.
44. V. Job et al., "Beliefs about Willpower Determine the Impact of Glucose on Self-Control," *Proceedings of the National Academy of Science* 110 (2013): 14837–42, doi:10.1073/pnas. 1313475110.
45. R. Kivetz and Y. Zhang, "Determinants of Justification and Self-Control," *Journal of Experimental Psychology* 135 (2006): 572–587, www.columbia.edu/~rk566/research/Justification_and_Self-Control.pdf.
46. Paul Tough, *How Children Succeed* (New York: Mariner Books, 2012).

CHAPTER 12:
THE POWER OF PARENTHOOD

1. "Jack Andraka Goes for the $10 Million X-Prize," YouTube, http://youtu.be/hoSoYf9aKAM.
2. "Facebook Parenting: For the Troubled Teen," YouTube, http://youtu.be/kl1ujzRidmU.
3. "A Magazine Is an iPad That Does Not Work," YouTube, http://youtu.be/aXV-yaFmQNk.

Acknowledgments

I'm grateful to the families I've seen in my practice, who've trusted me and shared their challenges, heartaches, and victories. I've learned from their resourcefulness and resilience.

Special thanks go to you, my readers, for your ongoing feedback and support. Your thoughtful comments and questions have kept me relevant and inspired.

I'm indebted to my agent, Robert Shepherd, for believing in this project from the start, generously sharing his expertise, and helping me clarify and develop my ideas. This book would not be a reality without him.

I want to acknowledge my editor, Beth Frankl, who's been indispensable to the project, providing encouragement, guidance, and context. I'm grateful to the staff at Shambhala, particularly Julie Saidenberg, Steven Pomije, and Julia Gaviria, and all those at Random House who've worked hard to put this book in your hands.

My heartfelt thanks go to Julia Cormano and Sarah French for reading and rereading chapters as I wrote and rewrote them and for the consistently helpful discussions that ensued. Their perspectives substantially improved and enriched this book. I'm grateful to many colleagues and friends for sharing stories and sparking ideas, most especially Jennifer Cormano, Larry Muirhead, Kelly Smith, and Dave deBronkart for their insightful and creative input.

I've relied on the assistance of my husband, Arthur Cormano. In addition to reading the manuscript, offering valuable suggestions, and helping with tasks ranging from solving word-processing glitches to producing the illustration, he took on the lion's share of domestic duties, smoothing my way and tirelessly cheering me on. Arthur, you are my superhero and I am forever grateful for your love. I feel blessed that you're my guy and that we share the privilege of parenting together.

Index

About the Author

Lucy Jo Palladino, PhD, has been a practicing psychologist for more than thirty-five years. Her expertise is the study of attention, with special interests in research, child development, and digital media. Her other books include the award-winning *Dreamers, Discoverers and Dynamos: How to Help the Child Who Is Bright, Bored, and Having Problems in School* and *Find Your Focus Zone: An Effective, New Plan to Defeat Distraction and Overload.* A mother of two, Dr. Palladino lives and works in Encinitas, California. You can follow her on Twitter @ljpalladino. Her website is lucyjopalladino.com.